THE TECHNIQUE
OF INDUSTRIAL ARCHAEOLOGY

THE INDUSTRIAL ARCHAEOLOGY
OF THE BRITISH ISLES

Series Editor: E. R. R. GREEN

Cornwall, by A. C. Todd and Peter Laws
Derbyshire, by Frank Nixon
The East Midlands, by David M. Smith
Galloway (South-west Scotland), by Ian Donnachie
Hertfordshire, by W. Branch Johnson
The Isle of Man, by L. S. Garrad, T. A. Bawden, J. K. Qualtrough, W. J. Scatchard.
The Lake Counties, by J. D. Marshall and M. Davies-Shiel
Lancashire, by Owen Ashmore
The Peak District, by Helen Harris
Scotland, by John Butt
Southern England (second edition, revised), by Kenneth Hudson

ASSOCIATED VOLUMES

The Bristol Region, by R. A. Buchanan and Neil Cossons
Dartmoor, by Helen Harris
Gloucestershire Woollen Mills, by Jennifer Tann
Stone Blocks and Iron Rails, by Bertram Baxter
The Tamar Valley (second impression, revised), by Frank Booker
The Techniques of Industrial Archaeology, by J. P. M. Pannell (second edition, revised by J. Kenneth Major)

OTHER INDUSTRIAL HISTORY

Brindley at Wet Earth Colliery: An Engineering Study, by A. G. Banks and R. B. Schofield
The British Iron and Steel Industry, by W. K. V. Gale
The Early Factory Masters, by Stanley D. Chapman
The Engineering Industry of the North of Ireland, by W. E. Coe
History of the Scottish Coal Industry, vol I *1700–1815*, by Baron F. Duckham
The History of Water Power in Ulster, by H. D. Gribbon

3
The Techniques of
INDUSTRIAL
ARCHAEOLOGY

2

J. P. M. PANNELL
Edited by
J. KENNETH MAJOR

4. 2nd ed.

DAVID & CHARLES: NEWTON ABBOT
1974

7

Printed in Great Britain
by Taylor Bros (Bristol) Limited
for David & Charles (Holdings) Limited
South Devon House Newton Abbot Devon

Contents

Introduction to Second Edition

IN the seven years since this book was first published the Industrial Archaeology movement has grown. Whereas in 1966 a small band of dedicated workers existed, there are now large Industrial Archaeology societies with many members. In some instances the workers are part-time enthusiasts, but in others they are associated with the universities. A lot of young people get their first taste of industrial archaeology when, as full-time students, they commence research and fieldwork as part of their course.

Again, in the seven years, there has been a large number of books published which, whilst covering the various aspects of individual subjects, or particular areas, have not added to the basic needs of the worker when he first starts as an industrial archaeologist. It is to fill this need that a new edition of this book has been published.

Kenneth Major, as editor of this edition, would like to thank Angus Buchanan, Lawrence Cameron, Douglas Hague and numerous other industrial archaeologists for their assistance and comments. Particular thanks must go to Helen Major for her care in preparing the manuscript for publication.

CHAPTER ONE

Introduction

THE importance of industrial archaeology as a subject for serious study has been increasingly recognized since the end of the 1939–45 war. Ideas on the scope of the subject are still fluid, however, in spite of attempts to define it. O. G. S. Crawford, that great field archaeologist, appreciated that, as a branch of anthropology, the subject of archaeology could not be confined within dates or periods, but represented the study of man through the physical remains of his past activities. If we accept this view, then industrial archaeology becomes a subject rather than a chronological subdivision of the main study—archaeology—and should include the archaeology of industry in all periods of the past. As, however, archaeologists of prehistoric, classical, medieval and other periods have included the industries of those times in their studies, it has been accepted that industrial archaeology starts where the already established periods end, or at the beginning of the Industrial Revolution.

This still leaves us with a wide tolerance in time, as it is by no means agreed when the Industrial Revolution began. Some authorities would put it as late at the mid-eighteenth century, when the beginnings of steam power offers a convenient date-line. Others attribute the Industrial Revolution to the migration from country to town, from village crafts to factory production, from the rule of parson and squire to that of the factory owner. It is already becoming evident that relics of any industrial activity from the sixteenth century onward are attracting the attention of students and are the subjects of papers and articles in journals interested in industrial archaeology.

The scope of the subject has been discussed by Kenneth Hudson in his book *Industrial Archaeology—an Introduction* (John Baker,

1963), and the reader of that work will quickly appreciate one fundamental difference between the archaeology of earlier periods and that of the Industrial Revolution—the vast growth in volume in printed and written matter, especially that connected with industry and commerce. The study of prehistoric man and his habits may only be pursued through the artifacts left behind; subsequent periods offer some slight support in the form of inscriptions, parchments and, later, books; but only in small proportion to the evidence left, mostly underground, in the form of man-made goods or structures. The industrial archaeologist has available an immense amount of written and printed material to supplement his study of the physical relics and, unless he is to be a mere measurer of stone, timber, or metal objects, he must relate his field studies to the documents which are contemporary with and relevant to his outdoor work. He will then find, before long, that he is an industrial historian in the fullest sense and that his contributions to knowledge of our industrial past are authoritative and, even if small, are very real.

Although, at the higher levels, archaeology progresses along lines pursued by a highly professional and devoted array of experts, it is —and has been for centuries—a study for the amateur. With increased leisure, more and more people are finding it brings that physical-cum-intellectual change of occupation which they need for full relaxation. For many such people, industrial archaeology affords much satisfaction; the amateur more often than not finds that he is an expert in one or more of the techniques required. The skills and professional knowledge of the architect, engineer and surveyor are obviously of value in the study of industrial buildings and machines; so are those of any craft workers and of people engaged in the handling or marketing of materials of construction or manufacture. Workers in such great industries as transport, power supply or mining may easily look backward into the development of their own calling, as in almost every instance their own knowledge and skill is based on that of their industrial ancestors.

Not only may those engaged in industry find that their special training helps them in the investigation of our industrial past. The special nature of industrial archaeology, linked as it is so closely with the written and printed records, needs the expert eye of the accountant, who can build up a picture of a long-dead business through its account books, or the civil servant, whose knowledge of Government procedures and publications makes him familiar with the development of the State and its links with industry. Teachers, in particular, may find the study of our industrial past, through its relics, an exciting way to illustrate the utility of many of the everyday subjects of the classroom. History, geography, mathematics, drawing and craft training may all be linked in the study of an extinct local industry, its rise, its days of prosperity and influence and its decline. The greater abundance of material available from the fairly recent past and its more evident influence on our present lives are likely to appeal to young students who may be uninspired by the activities of our more distant ancestors.

Whatever the daily avocation of the amateur industrial archaeologist, he will at some point in his field work or archive investigations need guidance in the elements of some skill which he does not possess. He may be able to measure a site or building, but not the machinery; or he could have a close knowledge of the business or personal side of a local industry, but be unable to relate the surviving examples of its products to the account books and correspondence files. The following chapters, while not pretending to close the gaps, are an attempt to help the industrial archaeologist who wishes to extend his skills and knowledge with the object of making his studies more complete. With the urgent need for recording the details of many vanishing industries, every worker in this field is able to make valuable contributions to our store of knowledge on our industrial origins. Suggestions for the most effective ways of contributing to the written and printed records are included in the later chapters in the hope that industrial archaeologists of amateur status will be encouraged to publish their facts and opinions at frequent intervals, for the interest and benefit of other workers.

Although the study of industrial history by the methods of archaeology has been described by the title 'industrial archaeology' for only a few years, the subject has been pursued for a much longer period. Transport has been studied by a number of enthusiastic societies and individuals who have published a great amount on the history of railways and canals. Groups such as the Railway & Canal Historical Society and the Cornish Engines Preservation Society do excellent, if specialized, work. Some artifacts of the mechanical age are almost worshipped by bodies who collect traction engines and vintage cars; yet, at the same time, vast tracts of mechanical engineering history are almost unexplored, particularly in the direction of machine tools. A start here has been made by the publication of *Tools for the Job* by L. T. C. Rolt (Batsford, 1965). This book represents a form of modern patronage which might well be emulated: it was sponsored by the machine tool group of firms centred on Charles Churchill & Company Limited to celebrate the centenary of the firm's foundation by Charles Churchill. Unfortunately, with the present-day urge to modernize, most manufacturers are more anxious to scrap fine examples of mid to late nineteenth-century machine tools than to sponsor attempts to record the details of their construction and use.

With the departure of machines of the hand-controlled variety and their replacement with new ones directed by computer and operated by hydraulic or other precision methods, the high degree of tactile and visual skill required by earlier machinists will be transferred to the machine. Unless we record in some way the nature of these skills, our descendants may wonder how our comparatively crude machines were used to produce goods of such great accuracy and reliability. Taking up the slack, or backlash, of a worn feed screw; adjusting a lathe to eliminate chatter; or even judging the 'feel' of calipers when comparing the diameters of two cylindrical objects; such things as this need to be transferred to film by some of the older generation of mechanics. Could not some of these, and similarly skilled people of other trades, now retired, be recorded by the BBC, the Science Museum and similar bodies, for the benefit of future industrial historians? In the meantime, ciné-camera and tape-recorder enthusiasts with a taste for the industrial arts might specialize in some of this work.

The scope of industrial archaeology is not necessarily confined to the production industries, transport, building and commercial activities on land. There may be a considerable overlap with transport by sea; for instance, the study of shipbuilding activities related to an area, or even to an individual yard, may extend to cover the subsequent history of the ships built. The Society for Nautical Research has for many years specialized in the maritime field but, just as the Newcomen Society furthers the study of what is now embraced under the general title of industrial archaeology, there seems to be no reason why nautical research in the archaeological sense should not be recognized as part of a whole. To some extent this is already being accepted as a working proposition and joint meetings of appropriate bodies are bound to provide a good interchange of ideas on subjects in the maritime world which require investigation and recording.

Kenneth Hudson, in his book already quoted, has stressed that in many fast-developing industries quite recently-established firms are already scrapping plant and methods adopted when their products were first put on to the market. This may have been only ten or even five years ago. The mass-production of transistors is a case in point: the transistor radio receiver has penetrated to every part of the world where radio programmes are receivable, but ten years ago the transistor was a laboratory device. It may be argued that modern firms keep the drawings and other records of their development types, but this is rarely the case. Much development, even today, is of the *ad hoc* kind; an idea sketched on the back of an envelope and transferred perhaps via a squared-paper sketch may find its way into a developing prototype as a piece of hardware without further record. We should keep in mind the hovercraft, which started as an old tin and a hair dryer. One of the most famous technical documents is the page, so often reproduced, from James Nasmyth's sketch book, which shows his steam hammer as an idea born in the engineer's mind almost complete before any other experimental work had been done. There may be sketch books of equal historical importance lying about today.

UNTRODDEN WAYS

Although many avenues of investigation are being followed, numerous branches of industrial archaeology remain to be explored. Any list of suggestions is bound to be no more than a representative sample, but consideration of a few may indicate the scope.

Public health may not appeal as a subject for study to everyone, but a great number of people are engaged in this essential service and there are professional institutions, university chairs and other evidence that the everyday problems of cleaning towns, sewage disposal and clean rivers are receiving proper attention. There is a considerable technical literature, but the history and archaeology of the subject has been, so far, somewhat neglected.

Many aspects of our civilization are dependent on complicated systems of distribution, and industries have grown up to solve the intricacies of getting food, clothing, building materials and even entertainment to the people who need them. The pipeline has to be kept neither clogged nor empty. The rise of the supermarket raises the question whether such changes in marketing may spread to the exclusion of small businesses, especially in towns. The cobbler's shop and the local bespoke tailor working over his business premises represent survivals of the old pattern of industry and need recording on film, tape and in documentation before they are gone. The printing trades and bookbinding are still carried on as local industries in parallel with greater undertakings. Even the local weekly paper is changing its pattern with offset lithography and other methods of modernization. What is happening to the old machines?

On a broader scale, the pattern of our local roads is now changing. Although this will remain substantially the same for generations to come, detailed alterations will make it more difficult in future years to separate roads in relation to their origins—trackway, Roman, Saxon, medieval, enclosure, toll, or even modern. Not only roads, but another aspect of our communications, minor coastal-port installations, are disappearing rapidly without trace, after centuries of use. In most of Britain's estuaries a great traffic was pursued between jetties, hards and similar landing places. The commercial aspects of this trade have, in recent years, been given some study by economic historians, but the physical remains of the actual landing places are in most cases unrecorded. The 1940 invasion precautions led to the destruction of many of our seaside pleasure piers, but there is still time to gather information about them. Many of the piers were built in the period 1850–1900, when cast iron piling was in vogue, and they represent an important step in the development of maritime construction.

Not only the pleasure piers, but other aspects of pleasure and recreation are worthy of recording, especially as in days of little leisure people tended to enjoy themselves more intensively. The technology of the theatre, of the early cinemas, and in particular of the fairground, offers a wide scope for study. Research into the manufacture of sports goods might appeal to those who enjoy using such equipment.

Another large field for study is the machinery for mass production starting with machine tools, particularly the lathe, the parent of them all. No other machine has the capacity of reproducing itself, but it is possible to design a lathe which will perform all the machining operations required to do so. Although there are enthusiasts who acquire vintage lathes, especially early ornamental types by Holtzapffel and others, there is little systematic work being done on recording the details of lathes, or indeed any machine tools. Not only the tools of the engineering production workshop require investigation, but those designed for the preparation and packing of our everyday requirements, from machines for making bread, biscuits and sweets, to cigarette-making and packing machinery. Much of this machinery has been developed on an *ad hoc* basis and some of the early examples are unlikely to be recorded by accurate drawings. The fascinating speed and complication of machines in this field lead to frequent obsolescence and replacements, making the task of recording often a matter of urgency.

The changing pattern of our towns is also bringing, every year, new tasks for industrial archaeologists. Street patterns are being altered to suit modern traffic; this involves not only demolition and rebuilding, but often the more important aspect of change of use. The ingenuity of man has always enabled him to adapt to a changing environment, and the conversion of buildings from one use to another is a practice which dates back to remote times. With the growth of towns and the tendency for residential areas to move outwards, the demand for shops and offices is met in the first instance by the alteration of houses to these purposes. It is a salutary exercise to walk along the shopping streets in many of our older towns, lifting the eyes above the uniformity of the standard and well-known shop fronts of the multiple stores, to see the great variety and character of the architecture in the buildings above. In some of our older towns, buildings of four or five different centuries will be found, disguised by false fronts like the dancers at a masked ball.

Not only shopping streets, but industrial areas offer much of interest to the student of social and economic change. The large warehouse buildings of dock areas, built to store goods unloaded from ships and awaiting distribution, or the reverse, are often now redundant through the rapid dispersal of cargoes on arrival, especially by road. Many have changed their function several times since the leisurely horse-and-cart days. With the closure of railways, the stations, goods sheds, offices and other buildings will be demolished or adapted. Even our rapidly expanding universities are changing their environments, houses becoming bank premises and offices, hotels turning into halls of residence and workshops into laboratories.

But this stress on buildings, machinery and their technology must not lead us from the main object of industrial—or indeed any—archaeology, the study of people and the lives they led. The evidence, however fascinating, must not be allowed to obscure this main theme: unless the study is related to mankind it is purposeless. History is of immense value to all who may, in any way, be responsible for the conduct of human affairs, but only if its findings relate the events and people. Industrial archaeology, as a part of the study of history, may be not only interesting in itself, but may also provide a standard of reference for present and future planners of our industrial life.

B

CHAPTER TWO

Written, Printed and Verbal Sources

THE student of industrial history and archaeology is fortunate in that, with few exceptions, the documentary records are written in the modern language of his country. Investigation of the social habits or the trade of earlier periods requires an expert knowledge of palaeography, of classical, oriental, or medieval languages, and of the specialized techniques required in dealing with fragile and almost undecipherable documents. For such reasons as these, the relationship between the archaeology of earlier periods and the written records, if there are any, becomes a highly professional activity.

When we come to the period of the Industrial Revolution, we have an entirely different set of circumstances. The arts of writing, calculating and drawing were not confined to the few. Correspondence was increasingly becoming a matter of communication between individuals without a third party intervening and simple accountancy was common to most small businesses. In spite of the inevitable inroads of time and the demands of two major wars on reusable paper, there still remains a vast quantity of record material which may be related to the artifacts of the period. No industrial archaelogist should ignore such material; without relating his field work to the documentary records, he is doing less than half a job. A good field study combined with archive research may, in the hands even of a comparative novice, add materially to our knowledge of the growth of an industry or community. Without the indoor work, the field work may be only a description of stones and timbers.

Printed and written documents may be found in the public collections, national and local, or they may be run to earth in the archives of great organizations such as the Coal, Gas, or Electricity Boards, of the railways and docks in Britain or abroad, in the professional institutions, in private hands and many other places. The Coal, Gas and Electricity Boards have accepted the principle that their pre-nationalization records should be transferred to local record offices. The importance of records is recognized officially by the central Government and by local authorities, not only in Britain but in most other countries. The principal offices for the preservation of public records in Britain are the Public Record Office in London, which contains records of England and Wales; the Scottish Record Office in Edinburgh and the Public Record Office of Northern Ireland in Belfast. In addition, records are maintained by some of the Government departments, such as the Customs & Excise, the National Maritime Museum and the Patent Office Library, and by many of the museums.

Many industrial archaeologists will, however, be more interested in the study of some special aspect of their own local industries; for, them, the sources of local records are all-important. In recent years, many of the county, city and county borough authorities have appointed officers to collect and care for the documentary history of their areas, not only of official activities, but also of business, industrial and even private affairs. These record offices are under the control of trained archivists who will be helpful in guiding the student of local history of any kind. Most of them provide facilities for the study of documents in their custody and many have equipment for document copying, microfilming or otherwise enabling the student to take copied material away for future use. In addition to the collections of counties and municipalities, the growth in recent years in the number and size of our universities and technical colleges has added new scope for the collection of material, especially local, of industrial, business, or scientific interest. Most of these sources are made available to the serious student, who will find not only documents of interest, but expert guidance on the literature of his special subject from people who are professionally trained in the booklore of history of all kinds. The same help may be found in provincial museums and in the collections held by such bodies as the Royal Institution of Cornwall at Truro and the Royal Institution of South Wales at Swansea, both in areas of great industrial interest.

A very useful guide to such sources is the list of *Record Repositories of Great Britain* published by Her Majesty's Stationery Office at frequent intervals. This list, while not including every source, gives the location, scope and facilities offered by most of the record offices in Great Britain.

PARLIAMENTARY PAPERS

In the broadest sense, the term Parliamentary Papers applies to all official publications connected with Parliament and its work. This immense field includes the record of Parliament's proceedings and debates, the reports of its own committees and of other bodies concerned with public affairs, and documents in great variety issued officially by Departments as part of their functions. In the more accepted sense, the term has a narrower and more precise meaning, that of documents brought before the House and included in one of its numbered series. These papers include what are popularly known as 'Blue Books', which may or may not have blue covers; for instance, a 'White Paper' is a blue book without a blue cover. The latter term has acquired a more specialized meaning since 1945, denoting a short statement on Government policy.

It will be appreciated that Parliament's paper records have built up during the course of centuries to a collection as great in volume as variety. From a clerkly record of its Acts, the records have grown to include not only the debates, but a mass of ancillary documents such as reports of committees, departmental papers, and annual or periodical reports of statutory bodies such as the National Coal Board or the Department of Scientific & Industrial Research. So great is the volume and so complicated are its variants that even experts flounder at times in the sea of paper.

This vast reservoir of material is an essential source of information to the social and economic historian and, unless his investigations are to be confined purely to excavation and measuring, the industrial archaeologist too is bound eventually to refer to one or other of the documents prepared under the aegis of Parliament. *A Guide to Parliamentary Papers* by Professor P. and Mrs G. Ford will provide preliminary guidance on what Parliamentary Papers are, how to find them and how to use them.

There are many classes of Parliamentary Papers which can be of use to the industrial archaeologist. The fieldworker who is following the route of a lost railway or canal should look first of all at the deposited plans contained with the papers collected prior to the passing of the appropriate Act. Deposited plans show the ownership of the lands through which the line had to pass, and since they had to be drawn up by the appointed engineer or his agent on the spot, their names will be shown on the plans. The committee papers and finally the Act will give the various points of debate and frequently show local prejudices and problems. Various manufactured items were often the subject of study by Commissions. These Commissions were held to ensure that satisfactory standards were maintained and that safety factors were observed. Frequently, too, these Commissions were held to examine the economic state of an industry. The extract given on the next page is from the evidence of I. K. Brunel to the Commission on the Use of Iron in Railway Bridges. This evidence shows the range of information to be obtained from the Commissioners' reports.

The proceedings of some Commissions continued for years, and the evidence, both oral and documentary, became so voluminous that the distribution of the reports became a serious financial problem. The Select Committee on Canals and Inland Waterways, set up in 1906, continued its investigation until 1911, the Report and

Appendices occupying twelve volumes of solid material. This report alone is of great value to the serious student of canal history, and many others of its kind are equally valuable in other fields of study. The practice of printing oral evidence in full was discontinued as a result of the need for economy during the 1914–18 war.

Evidence from the Report of the Commissioners appointed to inquire into the application of Iron to Railway Structures. (Command Paper No. 1123–1849)
Extract. Thursday, April 13, 1848.
        LORD WROTTESLEY, in the Chair.
        Isambard Kingdon (sic) *Brunel Esq.*, examined.
1143. (*Chairman*) Your are a civil engineer?—I am.
1144. Would you like to mention any of the principal works in which you have been engaged?—I have been engaged principally upon railways in the south-west of England, the Great Western Railway and the other railways connected with it and the works in the immediate neighbourhood and also in one or two suspension bridges, which although not railway bridges, may be considered as works connected with the present inquiry.
1145. Have you turned your attention to the chemical constituents of iron, or to the effect which variations in them produce on the strength of iron?—Not sufficiently to consider myself at all informed upon the subject.
1146. Can you give any information at all upon the subject?—I have endeavoured to possess myself of such information as was within my reach; but the result, I am sorry to say, is that I consider myself quite ignorant upon the subject.
1147. Of the various irons produced by the furnaces of England, Scotland and Wales, which do you prefer for girder bridges?—My experience has been mostly with the Welch and Staffordshire iron and therefore I should not like to speak very generally with respect to the Scotch. My preference, from what little judgement I can form with respect to others, has been for the Welch and Staffordshire.
1148. What mixtures of iron do you prefer for large castings?—I have endeavoured to have a very small proportion of the hot-blast iron from the results of my observations.
1149. A small proportion?—Yes, a very small proportion.
1150. Have you any objection to hot-blast generally?—My prejudices are against hot-blast and that is about all I can say upon it from the general result of my observations.

ANNUAL REPORTS OF DEPARTMENTS AND STATUTORY BODIES

Not only are the reports of Government Departments such as the Department of the Environment, with its sections of Transport and Works, and the Department of Trade valuable sources of information on matters of trade, communication and industry, but also Parliamentary bodies set up to perform special functions issue reports which provide information on particular subjects. These range from the reports of official laboratories such as those for Hydraulics or Road Research, to the reports of the Inspector of Factories, the British Broadcasting Corporation and the Council of Industrial Design. Sources such as these will aid the industrial archaeologist in relating his special work to other activities and to the pattern of life in the community during the period under his review.

COMPANY RECORDS

Most British companies of any age possess some records of their proceedings, but they have no archive-preserving tradition as many European and American companies have. Sometimes a selection of the older archives has been rescued from official destruction by an interested employee or has escaped by being overlooked. Most companies refuse access to their records, although the few large companies which have appointed archivists are notable exceptions. The most usual excuse is an assertion that everything was destroyed during the war, in a disastrous fire, or at an amalgamation. Patience and a tactful persistence will often overcome this attitude, so that when the company is assured of the student's good intentions every record may be shown to him.

As might be expected, most of the records are account books, journals, day books, waste books, ledgers and the like. These tend to be preserved more readily than anything else, but are extremely rare for dates earlier than 1800. When the firm's work was not standardized, job books and plans may also be found, as they would have been preserved for repeat orders or repair and maintenance purposes. Even more valuable are the letter books because they are not formal records, but personal documents which give us information about the characters of those involved. However, the student will be lucky if he finds more than a dozen volumes for a particular company.

The records of companies which have passed into public ownership are usually better preserved. The Northam Bridge Company and the Floating Bridge Company which were bought by Southampton Corporation transferred many of their records. Even so the clerk to Northam Bridge Company retained some. Perhaps the best preserved company records are those of businesses which went bankrupt. Before the Bankruptcy Court was established in 1844, there were local commissions of bankruptcy whose clerk was often clerk of the peace. Where the commissioners' records have survived amongst the quarter-sessions records, they include account books and the examinations of the creditors and debtors. Even where the company was not actually made bankrupt, its records can often be discovered. The Southampton & Salisbury Canal Company archives were faithfully preserved by its last clerk although it only existed fifteen years and never made a penny of profit for its shareholders.

PERIODICAL LITERATURE

The periodical press, ranging from daily and weekly newspapers of national and local circulation, to specialist journals covering almost every aspect of human interest and activity, offers such an overwhelming source of information to the industrial archaeologist that he often fails to use it to fullest advantage.

Major developments in science and technology receive due attention in the great national newspapers, and bound volumes of *The*

Times are kept in most of the bigger public libraries. The pages devoted to finance, commerce and industry will provide useful source material for dating the origins and growth of whole industries as well as individual firms. So will the advertising pages, and these should not be neglected in any class of periodical.

The local daily press is able to cover in more detail those aspects of industry which affect its community. Our Victorian ancestors were great readers of the local weekly papers, whose editorial staffs endeavoured to fill their columns with close-printed descriptions of local activities, verbatim reports of speeches, columns of correspondence and, not least, advertisements of all kinds. To study such sources may seem to be a daunting task, but with practice the reader is able to scan the columns and pages quickly to pick out items of interest and importance.

The weekly, monthly and quarterly journals, specializing in most aspects of individual and corporate activity, are probably more easily worked through. From the early volumes of the *Gentleman's Magazine* and its later counterpart, the *Mechanic's Magazine*, the student may find articles and correspondence reflecting the industrial progress of the late eighteenth and early nineteenth centuries. As the pace of the Industrial Revolution increased, specialized journals such as *The Engineer* and *Engineering* came into being. The standard of illustrations in these magazines has always been high and they provide a constant review of the state of industry at all times from the mid-nineteenth century.

Journals for the amateur enthusiast are of more recent origin, but have multiplied greatly in number during the present century whilst at the same time their content has developed in quality. This is largely due to the increase of leisure which, leading to the acquisition of greater skills and thus to a more critical discernment by the readers, has raised the standard of articles submitted by amateur practitioners of all kinds to their hobby magazines. An example is the *Model Engineer* which, while having always given useful information on workshop practice current at the time of publication, now includes a substantial number of articles on engineering history and early technology. Of all such publications, the *Transactions* of the Newcomen Society are probably the most valuable to the industrial archaeologist who is interested in the history of manufacture, transport and engineering.

DIRECTORIES

The fieldworker in any chosen subject will find a great deal of the information which he needs, when looking for the sites occupied by an industry, in the many national and regional directories which are available. These directories first appeared at the beginning of the Industrial Revolution, and have been published at irregular intervals ever since.

There are two good bibliographies of those directories which appeared before 1856: C. W. F. Goss, *The London Directories 1677–1855*, and Jane E. Norton, *Guide to the National and Provincial Directories*. These bibliographies should be the starting point for the student who wishes to use directories.

One of the earliest projects for a national directory was based on *Bailey's Directory of London and the Principal Towns North of the Trent*, published in 1781 under the patronage of John Stephenson, a Hull merchant. In 1787, Bailey started on a general directory of England, in parts, but the only part known to have survived is the one for Bristol. Bailey claimed to have visited every house and business listed in his directories, and this claim applies to his earlier *Western and Midland Directory*, published in 1784. This was printed by Pearson and Rollason in Birmingham, and includes alphabetical and commercial lists for a number of towns.

Peter Barfoot and John Wilkes, who published the *Universal British Directory* between 1790 and 1798, were not scrupulous in checking lists of names. In fact, they compiled their directories by using the lists, unchecked, which had appeared in other directories.

Agents were employed to tout for subscribers and to supply the lists of householders.

The *Triennial Directory* by William Holden and Thomas Underhill must have been even more unreliable. It was published for the large sum, by the standards of those days, of £1 19s 6d with a print order of 11,000 copies. Its unreliability stems from the fact that it was pirated from the *Universal British Directory*. Holden set out to change the style of his directory from an alphabetical to a classified listing. In 1814 he published a volume on the textile trade, but died before the project had got very far. On his death, the compilation passed to Underhill, who reverted to an alphabetical classification, but left a trade classification in certain towns. This series ceased in 1822.

The best known directories are Kelly's. Francis Kelly was an official in the London General Post Office and he bought the copyright of the *Post Office London Directory* in 1836. By 1845 his business as a publisher was firmly established, and he launched a series of provincial directories. The six Home Counties were the first volumes. Kelly did not reissue earlier directories, but from the start set out to present up-to-date information from his own surveys on the ground. The series, which contains county as well as local volumes, is still in production today. In Kelly's directories, the standard format of alphabetical listing with a trades listing in each town has been maintained consistently since the earliest times. The historical and topographical descriptions which introduce each locality are also useful.

A series of directories which started in 1817 with a directory of Leeds was published by Edward Baines. This was taken over by William Parson, and later William White joined the company. This association continued until 1830, after which time William White took over the management. Figure 1 is a page from William White's *History, Gazetteer and Directory of Devonshire*, which shows the population and trades of Crediton. Unlike Kelly, the volumes were are attended by about 140 boys and 90 girls; and 55 of them are clothed at the expense of the charity. They are all instructed gratuitously, and provided with books and stationery. The master has a yearly salary of £72, and the mistress £20, and they have the free use of a house adjoining the school.

DUNN'S SCHOOL.—*Samuel Dunn*, in 1794, left to the "Governors of Crediton," £600 in trust to pay the yearly proceeds thereof to a schoolmaster for teaching writing, navigation, mathematics, &c., to at least six boys of the Church of England; preference to be given to those of the names of Dunn and Harris. This legacy was laid out in the purchase of £630 new four per cent. stock, for the dividends of which a schoolmaster teaches 12 boys of Crediton, in the house at Bowdon hill, which was formerly appropriated to the English School.

CREDITON DIRECTORY.

Those marked 1, are in East Town; 2, High street; 3, Market street; 4, North street; and 5, in Parliament street.

The POST-OFFICE is at Mr. Francis Shute's, High street. Letters despatched at 45 minutes past 12 in the afternoon, and at 10 minutes past 7 in the evening, via Exeter; and to Bideford, Barnstaple, &c., every morning.

Backwell Saml. inspr. of weights and measures
1 Badcock John, wine merchant, &c.
2 Baker Rev James, (Independent)
Bent Mrs Emily, Penton cottage
Bishop Wm. earthenware dealer
Blagden Peter, gent. Mill street
4 Boxer Robert, news agent
2 Brown Mr Saml. & 4 Mrs My. Ann
Buller Jas. Wentworth, Esq. *Downes*
1 Burdge Mr Wm. || Berry Mr John
Cade Thos. veterinary surgeon
Carthew John, miller, *Four Mills*
Cleave Benj. sen. and jun. Esqrs. *Newcombes*
Davy and Sons, linen, sacking, &c. manufacturers, *Fordton Mills*
Dawe Mrs Annette, Market street
Day Rev Saml. Phillips, (Indpt.)
2 *Devon and Cornwall Bank;* open Saturday
1 Deans Rev James, M.A. curate
5 Dicker Rt. cabinet mkr. par. clerk, and agt. to Western Provdt. Instn.
Drake John, gent. *Winswood House*
1 Drake Misses Chtte. and Charity
Dutchman Hewson, R.N. High st
2 Francis Mr Wm. and Mr James
Francis Mrs Eliz., Blagden place
Francis Miss, Palace cottage
1 Furse Wm. coal agent
Gorwyn Mr Richard Lambert
2 Gover Jas. brush and bellows mkr
2 Gover John, brush & bellows mkr
Guest John, supervisor, High st
Guppy Jane, beerhouse, High st
2 Hall Mr Saml. || Halse Mr N.W.
1 Haycraft Daniel, fellmonger
1 Hayes Wm. organist
Hippesley J. H. Esq. *Fulford Park*
2 Hoard Wm. A. machine maker
Holman Capt. Charles, High st
Hookway Giles, gentleman
Hugo Stephen, gent. High street
2 Kelland Mrs || Kingdon Mrs
4 Langabeer Jas. cheesemonger
Leach Rev George, (Wesleyan)
Leach Wm. Comyns, master of work- [house
Lee Fras. court bailiff
Lightfoot Mrs and Miss, East town
McCombe Rev Alex. (Unitarian)
2 Madge Wm. supt. of Gas works
2 Madge Mr Thos.||Pearse Mr Wm.
Melhuish Mrs., Fair Park cottage
2 Norrish Abm. tallow chandler
2 Park John, clothes cleaner
Prickman Mr Ts. & Mrs. Blagden pl
2 Renwick Capt. Ts. & Rev. Ts., B.A.
Roberts Mrs Sarah, North street
Rowe Rev Saml., M.A. Vicarage
Rowe Richd. starch manufacturer
Rudall Francis, gent. *Palace*
Rudall Miss Ann, East town
Shute Fras. post master, High st
3 Smith Mrs || Snow Mrs Chtte.
2 Taylor Mr John || Tarrant Mr Wm.
2 Thomas John, china, glass, &c. dlr
5 Tremlett Mrs B. || Temple Mrs

Fig. 1. The page referring to Crediton from William White's *History, Gazetteer and Directory of Devonshire*

not produced to a uniform standard, and the best volumes are those for Devonshire, Essex, Norfolk, Suffolk and Yorkshire.

In using directories the fieldworker should be careful to observe the following points. Not everybody or every tradesman was listed; in some cases payment was involved for an entry and therefore some people were unable or unwilling to pay. The publication date was often two or three years after the survey was carried out, and the dates of publication were extremely irregular. However, if one wished to pursue the changes in an industry, then a series of year-by-year lists prepared from a directory would give a reasonable guide to the changes in that industry. Directories should, however, be used only as a rough guide to the sites which existed because of their inability to list everything. For example, a county list of watermills taken from Kelly would not list those mills which were on private property and, though working, did not trade.

GUIDE-BOOKS

National and local directories can give a great deal of guidance to local studies and to industrial archaeology. As soon as journeys of exploration became fashionable, in the eighteenth century, guide-books were published for tourists in search of the picturesque. Although the landed gentry went abroad in their youth on the Grand Tour, in staid middle age they went to the fashionable resorts of Bath, Brighton, Derbyshire and the Lake District. As they travelled the roads they used guides which indicated what could be seen on either side of the road such as *Paterson's Roads*, *Kearsley's Traveller's Entertaining Guide Through Great Britain*, or *Cary's Great Roads*. These guides described the various places one came to on each road, and gave the distance from the last place and the distance from the start of the journey. The various large houses which were close to the route were described for two reasons: to make more people buy the volumes, and to enable people to find the houses, for in this period, travellers were often welcome to call when passing the house of an acquaintance. This was necessary to enable the horses to be rested, and it also meant that friends and relatives could meet. Because of the difficulties of travel, such meetings did not take place very frequently.

A page from *Paterson's Roads* is illustrated in Figure 2 on page 32, and shows a stretch of the London–Holyhead road. Reference is made to Matthew Boulton, James Watt and the industries of Birmingham. In Wednesbury you will see that there was Pit Coal which was taken by canal to Birmingham. The traveller is also told that he has crossed the Birmingham Canal just to the north of Wednesbury. The road connections are also marked.

The information contained in this sort of guide is well worth reading. The reference to Hull in *Kearsley's Traveller's Guide* is typical of the style and description used in these guides:

HULL, *Yorkshire*, or KINGSTON-UPON-HULL, is seated on the north side of the river Humber, and is a handsome, large town, with two parish churches. It is fortified, and is the first town that shut its gates against Charles the First; but its fortifications are now inconsiderable, while its commerce is increased so much, that it is, perhaps, the fourth port in the kingdom. Its situation is extremely advantageous, for, besides its communication with the Yorkshire rivers and canals, it has access also by the Humber to the Trent and its branches. The foreign trade is chiefly to the Baltic, but it has also regular traffic with the southern parts of Europe, and with America. More ships are sent hence to Greenland than from any other port, except London. The coasting trade is very considerable. Among the public buildings are the Trinity-house, for the relief of seamen and their widows, and an exchange. The noble stone bridge over the river to Holderness was rebuilt in 1787, and consists of fourteen arches. *Cross Keys, and Saracen's Head.*

In addition to the guide-books to the roads, there were road maps. The first and perhaps best known of these is John Ogilby's *Britannia* of 1675. This map is a series of strips which show the principal roads with the distances marked on them, and the associated landmarks drawn in their correct positions. The various changes in direction were indicated by a compass rose. Ogilby had successors such as Emanuel Bowen who wrote *Britannia Depicta or*

Ogilby Improved in 1720, and, in the railway era, books such as *The Grand Junction and the Liverpool and Manchester Railway Companion* of 1837.

Various localities which were attractive to tourists produced guide-books which described the area without paying undue attention to the roads. These frequently listed all the inns, but their attention to detail was best shown in their descriptions of local viewpoints, historic houses and, in many cases, industries. In the Lake District, Jonathan Otley produced *A Concise Description of the English Lakes*. The 1830 edition contains this description of the Borrowdale plumbago mine.

> . . . An old level, which was re-opened in 1769, was found to have been cut through very hard rock, without the help of gunpowder; and a kind of pipe vein which had produced a great quantity of wad (plumbago) having been pursued to the depth of one hundred yards or more, much inconvenience was experienced in working it: to obviate which, in 1798, an adit or level was begun in the side of the hill, which at the length of 220 yards communicates with the bottom of the former sinking; since which time the works have been carried on internally through various ramifications; a survey of which was made a few years ago by the late Mr. Farey. Through the principal level the water now passes off, and the produce and rubbish are brought out upon a railway in a small waggon, and over its mouth a house is built, where the workmen are undressed and examined as they pass through it on leaving their work.

Though the adit now contains conventional mine rail, the description is still valid with the ruins of the house at the mouth. The rail was plate rail, and a piece was found in the tip outside the adit, after a cloudburst in 1966.

In the same area, Wordsworth was the author of a guide-book, and there have been dozens of guide-books since. Perhaps the best series of Lake District guides which can interest the industrial archaeologist are the latest—Wainwright's *A Pictorial Guide to the Lakeland Fells*. The seven pocket volumes indicate most of the visible industrial sites on the fells. Such guides can be good bedtime reading for the industrial archaeologist.

122] ROADS measured from TYBURN TURNPIKE.

l. to Moreton in the Marsh, 9 m.; r. to Warwick $14\frac{3}{4}$.		
Newbold - - - -	2	$86\frac{3}{4}$
Cross the river Stour.		
Alderminster - - -	2	$88\frac{3}{4}$
BridgeTown, *Warwick.*	4	$92\frac{3}{4}$
r. to Banbury $19\frac{1}{2}$ *m.; and to Kineton* 11.		
Cross the Avon river.		
* *STRATFORD ON AVON* - - - -	$\frac{1}{2}$	$93\frac{1}{4}$
r. to Warwick 8 *m.; l. to Alcester* $7\frac{3}{4}$.		
Stratford on Avon Canal	$5\frac{1}{4}$	$98\frac{1}{2}$
Wotton Waven - -	$\frac{3}{4}$	$99\frac{1}{4}$
* *HENLEY IN ARDEN* - - - - -	2	$101\frac{1}{4}$
Cross the canal.		
* Hockley Heath - -	5	$106\frac{1}{4}$
r. to Warwick 10 *m.*		
Monksford Street - -	$1\frac{3}{4}$	108
Shirley Street - - -	3	111
3 *m. farther, r. to Solihull* $4\frac{1}{2}$ *m.; thence to Warwick* $13\frac{1}{4}$.		
Camphill - - - -	$4\frac{1}{4}$	115
A little farther, r. to Coventry 16 *m.; l. to Alcester* $18\frac{1}{4}$.		
Cross the Tame river.		
* *BIRMINGHAM* -	$1\frac{1}{4}$	$116\frac{1}{2}$
r. to Coleshill $8\frac{3}{4}$ *m.; to Tamworth* $14\frac{3}{4}$; *to Sutton* $7\frac{1}{2}$; *and thence to Lichfield* $8\frac{1}{2}$; *l. to Bromesgrove* 13; *to Kidderminster* 17; *to Stourbridge* $12\frac{1}{4}$; *and to Dudley* 10.		
Hockley Brook - - -	$1\frac{1}{2}$	118
r. to Walsall 7 *m.; thence to Wolverhampton* 7.		
Soho, *Staffordshire* -	$\frac{1}{2}$	$118\frac{1}{2}$
New Inn - - - -	1	$119\frac{1}{2}$
Sandwell Green - -	1	$120\frac{1}{2}$
Bromwich Heath - -	1	$121\frac{1}{2}$
A mile farther, l. to Bilston by Horsley Heath 5 *m.; r. to*		
WEDNESBURY - -	3	$124\frac{1}{2}$
r. to Walsall 3 *m.; and to Bilston by Darlaston* $3\frac{1}{2}$.		
Cross the Birmingham canal.		

Newbold. Beyond, on *r*, at Lower Eatington, Evelyn Shirley, Esq.; on *l*, Talton Hill, Miss Parker.

Alderminster. Near two miles beyond, on *l*, Oscot Park, Mrs. West.

Stratford on Avon. Half a mile beyond, Clopton House, R. Williams, Esq. Stratford on Avon is remarkable as the birth place of Shakespeare, who was buried here in 1616, and his Monument is in the Church. Trinity Church is a very ancient structure.

Wotton Waven. On *r*, Wotton Hall, Sir Edward Smythe, Bart.

Henley in Arden. On *l*, Barrells House, Robert Knight, Esq.

Hockley Heath. A mile before, on *l*, Umberslade, Lady Archer.

Birmingham is celebrated for its manufacture of Hardwares; such as Metal Buttons, Buckles, Plated Goods of all kinds, Japanned and Paper Ware, &c. These Goods are dispersed throughout the kingdom, and exported in large quantities to foreign countries.

Hockley Brook. On *r*, Packwood House, F. Dilkes, Esq.; Soho, late Matthew Boulton, Esq. This gentleman, in conjunction with James Watt, Esq., has constructed some of the most complete and powerful steam engines in Europe; particularly one at Hawkesbury Colliery, near Coventry, with several others in Staffordshire, Shropshire, Warwickshire, Cornwall, &c.

Sandwell Green. On *r*, Sandwell Park, Earl of Dartmouth; and near it, Sir Jervoise Clerk Jervoise, Bart.

Wednesbury. A great quantity of excellent Pit Coal is dug here, with which Birmingham is supplied by means of a canal. Here is likewise a species of Iron Ore, used to make Nails, Horse Shoes, &c.

Fig 2. A page from *Paterson's Roads*

This monumental and marathon work can be one of the principal sources of information to the industrial archaeologist. Dedicated to Queen Victoria, the first volumes were produced in the last years of her reign, and the series has been growing to the present day, though not every county has even yet been covered. The VCH, as it has become known to its users, demonstrates the change of approach to history during the years of the present century, with its gradual alteration of stress from church and manorial life to an appreciation of society as a whole, including the industries and day-to-day life of the people.

Among the earliest volumes issued were those covering the County of Hampshire, volume one being dated 1901 and volume four, 1911. Commencing with a comprehensive survey of the county as a whole, its geology, botany, zoology, and its general history from Roman times, the volumes continue with the more detailed histories of its ecclesiastical and scholastic organizations and of its greatest single geographical unit, the New Forest. The two last volumes contain the detailed histories of the parishes, grouped in hundreds, and the limited scope of these histories may be judged by that of the parish of Funtley, in the hundred of Titchfield, which deals entirely with manorial matters, making no mention of the existence of Henry Cort who, in this parish, developed some of the greatest advances in the techniques of working iron. Yet in spite of the omissions, even the earliest volumes of the VCH contain much interest and information for the industrial archaeologist.

The Hampshire volumes may be compared with the more recent treatment of the County of Warwick, of which volume seven, devoted to Birmingham, covers the period of that city's industrial development, especially from the early eighteenth century. Although it is planned on similar lines to the earlier volumes of the VCH,

C

with a general historical survey of the area, this is followed by more specialized histories of its industries and social activities, each supplemented by details, with dates, of the organizations and buildings associated with them. Although churches are not overlooked, the illustrations naturally include a greater proportion of pictures of the industries and social life of the city. One of the features of the VCH is its abundance of footnotes giving the documentary sources, and most industrial archaeologists will find, in these references, much of the reading needed to authenticate the history of any part of the activity of the city, especially that which has influenced its growth.

DIARIES AND JOURNALS

A dedicated diarist may in the course of his or her lifetime write forty or fifty annual volumes of notes on the daily round of his environment. Many such diaries are known to have survived; a large proportion of these are in public or private collections. The value to the industrial archaeologist of such sources of information does not need to be stressed, but it may be difficult to know where to look for diaries covering the place and period under review. A useful guide may be found in *British Diaries 1442–1942* compiled by William Matthews. This bibliography of diaries by all kinds of people includes notes on such matters as the profession of the diarist and the nature of his approach—that is, whether it is strictly personal and family, or whether it includes, as in most cases, comments concerning his trade or profession. The period of the diaries is given and information on where they may be found.

Diaries listed in this bibliography include a large number by people connected with the Industrial Revolution, such as John Urpeth Rastrick, whose diaries for the years 1806- 1853 are preserved in the library of the University of London. Rastrick was a great engineer and designer of works in iron; the Chepstow road bridge over the Wye is one of his notable works still in use. Two series of diaries by members of the Stevenson family are noted, those from 1807 to 1811 by Robert, the builder of the Bell Rock Lighthouse, and David, whose diaries from 1852 to 1874 record his business life and work as a railway engineer. Similar sets of diaries listed cover almost every kind of activity and are from people in all social classes.

While some people keep a daily diary, with each day's doings recorded on a page reserved for them, others prefer to record their activities in journal form, giving space according to the frequency and importance of events. Such records may be of even greater value, as the writer is not tempted to be unduly brief in order to pack a full day's events on to a single page. An engineer friend of the author kept a journal for most of his life, recording with equal fidelity the technical details of his interesting work, the activities of his local cricket team and those of his family. Such a record, put away for fifty years or more, will prove to be full of the material of social history.

Even one or two odd volumes of a diary may bring new light on some subject of interest, as did two volumes found recently in an office at Plymouth which had been for many years the Divisional Engineer's Office of the Great Western Railway. This office took over the documents of the South Devon Railway and the Cornwall Railway when they became part of the Great Western, the engineer of both lines at that time being P. J. Margary. These diaries (Figure 3) were written by Margary in 1845 and 1847, when he was a young man and Brunel's resident engineer on the South Devon Railway (the atmospheric) during its construction. Apart from their technical interest, they convey information about the life of a young engineer of those days in a manner not to be found elsewhere. In these days of holidays with pay, it seems incredible that apart from Sundays, Good Friday and Christmas Day, Margary has no holiday in either of those two years. He also suffered, as does his equivalent

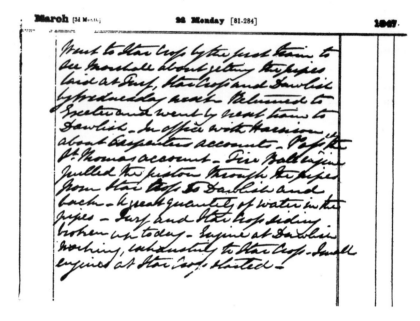

Fig 3. Page of diary of P. J. Margary, resident engineer to
I. K. Brunel on the South Devon (atmospheric) Railway

today, from local hooligans who removed his setting-out pegs, from
undisciplined workmen—and from the weather.

PROCEEDINGS OF SOCIETIES

Guilds, societies and institutions of all kinds for the protection
and education of members of trades and professions have existed
for many centuries. Today, few if any groups of individuals having
common interests refrain from publishing some sort of papers
arising from their activities. From the early days of the Royal
Society down to the present time there has been a constant flow of
printed records of invention, innovation and the discussions there-

on. From a trickle, the flow has increased to a spate far greater than any one person can assimilate; a vast reservoir of information is available in this form for the keen student to dive into when searching for information on almost any subject. Many of the major societies produce indexes at intervals of a number of years, and judicious inquiry will often save weeks of labour in searching for clues.

It is customary in many societies for presidential addresses to be delivered and fortunately some such addresses consist of a review of that aspect of the trade or profession in which the eminent holder of the presidential office is an acknowledged expert. Such sources are most valuable as they frequently start off with a historical review of the subject with the comments and criticisms of high authority.

TEXTBOOKS AND PAMPHLETS

The accumulated knowledge made available in the proceedings of learned societies and the reports of research organizations eventually becomes too unwieldy for the individual to find and absorb. So to reduce this knowledge to a convenient form, a textbook or books materialize. From the beginning of the nineteenth century, a great number of such books were written to cope with the demand for information on a wide range of subjects. Some became classics, many were valuable, some were of little use at all. The student of any branch of industrial archaeology will not be wasting his time by taking an occasional browse through the dustier basement shelves of second-hand bookshops. Not all the treasures have found their way yet into the more expensive specialists' catalogues. Professor W. G. Hoskins, in one of his valuable books, says that no local historian should fear getting his feet wet; this advice is equally valuable to the industrial archaeologist who, along with the local historian, should not mind getting his fingers grubby.

Many textbooks of the nineteenth century reflect the long working hours and low wages of the period in the lavish provision of illustrations. The reproduction of photographs by the half-tone process was not yet available, but high-quality steel, copper and wood engravings were included in plenty. These engravings are usually in great detail and show accurately the technical practices and skills of the period.

CATALOGUES

The value and interest of catalogues appears to have been neglected by the principal libraries, but this kind of printed material can provide in a compact form information which, if available elsewhere at all, is dispersed and often incomplete. During the nineteenth and early twentieth centuries, printed matter was cheap to produce and manufacturers in search of markets took pains to issue elaborate catalogues. Although the paper famine of two major wars reduced their chances of survival, the top shelves of book stores and other out-of-the-way places can yield such treasure trove.

Among the goods regularly advertised in catalogue form were engineering products, builders' hardware, foundry goods, textiles, tools and equipment of most trades; even large civil engineering works were, and still are, included in advertising literature ranging from large and expensive cloth-bound volumes to single-page reprints of magazine articles. One or more major libraries could with advantage be devoted to collecting this kind of printed record, much of which disappears without trace.

Many of the great constructional firms produced catalogues or their equivalent in publicity material as, for instance, the Crumlin Viaduct Works. Established originally at Crumlin on the Pontypool branch of the Taff Vale Railway for the fabrication of the ironwork of the great Crumlin Viaduct, this works proceeded to manufacture standard components for the erection, in all parts of the world, of bridges, piers, wharves, sheds and the like (Figure 4). The company's catalogues give a clear indication of the state of structural engineering about the mid-nineteenth century. About half a century later, the Hennebique system of reinforced concrete was rapidly coming into use and, in 1905, that company produced a catalogue which not only explained in considerable detail the principles and advantages of the system, but also described with illustrations and drawings almost all the structures built by the system up to that date. The Coignet, Considere, Kahn and other systems emulated this practice and their combined efforts must have included practically all reinforced concrete works built about that time.

Fig 4. Suspension footbridge made at Crumlin Viaduct Works

These catalogues not only provided complete details of the products, but in many cases told the early history of the firms concerned. Complete with portraits of chairmen and other personalities, they frequently gave details of the progressive growth of the factory or mill, information which in many cases is unobtainable in any other form.

HOUSE JOURNALS AND INSTRUCTIONAL LITERATURE

From the straightforward catalogue has developed the more modern house journal, which usually combines news of the firm's achievements and of the people it employs. Selectively preserved and indexed, even the records of wedding and retirement presentations, the clocks and transistor radios, will interest future social historians, as the description of the firm's latest equipment installed in factory or port in Japan, Peru, or South Africa will interest the industrial archaeologist.

Another prolific form of record material is the books, pamphlets and leaflets issued to the purchasers of machinery and similar manufactured goods. This may be anything from an expensively produced and illustrated maintenance handbook to a tie-on tag with instructions on washing a new synthetic fabric. The growing practice of wrapping or packing goods at the factory, often in cartons which include instructions for use, is a social phenomenon which needs recording in adequate but not extravagant detail.

CONTRACT DOCUMENTS

The practice of organizing works of construction by contracts is one of ancient origin, dating back to Roman times and perhaps earlier. The contract system as we know it today applied to works of civil engineering owes its main features to Thomas Telford who, by the careful selection of his contractors and by complete impartiality in interpreting the contract documents, was able to avoid serious disputes throughout his career.

A set of documents for a construction contract or one for installing mechanical or electrical plant usually consists of the drawings, specification, bill of quantities and the general conditions of contract. The last-named is fairly lengthy, having a number of clauses couched in clear but precise legal language which define the conditions under which both parties agree to work. It is the result of many decades of experience in contract work and, although its incorporation in a contract is not a guarantee that arguments will not arise, it greatly reduces the chance of litigation. The other three documents are meant to be read together and show the intentions of the engineer who designed the work, usually in great detail. Any set of contract documents is therefore of great value to the industrial archaeologist who must, however, use it cautiously as the finished work may not be in exact accordance with it. Ideally, a set of drawings showing modifications should be prepared at the end of the job, and this is sometimes done. More frequently this is never achieved, and contract drawings should always be suspect to some degree.

The submission of tenders for a contract is usually accompanied or followed by a priced bill of quantities, in which the details of the work are separately priced. This enables modifications to be incorporated in the work at a price adjustment which is fair to both parties. Priced bills of quantities are extremely valuable documents for the economic historian who can compare money values between different places and times.

VERBAL SOURCES

Much information about our industries may be obtained from the recollections of the older generation of workers in those industries. This applies particularly to such matters as the methods of operating unusual machinery, the layout and use of factory buildings, biographical details of the owners, or management organization and methods. Even allowing for the frailty of human memory, such help given by people who actually worked in a factory or mill, long since disused, can often suggest new lines of approach to an investigation. The quotation of verbal material should always be clearly stated as such, with the conditions leading to its acquisition, so that later students may know the status and degree of intelligence of the informant, whether the information was first or second hand, and the lapse of time between the events and their recording. The possibility that the volunteer of verbal information may be in possession of, or have access to, photographs, letters, old newspapers and such written or printed material, should not be overlooked. Even better, such a willing helper may be persuaded to walk through the works, mill, or railway yard, a procedure which is almost certainly stimulating to the memory.

In almost every case where verbal information is volunteered, a tape-recorder is obviously likely to be useful. A few people of the older generation may dry up in the presence of such an instrument, but more often its production will stimulate the flow of reminiscence. The small self-contained transistor type of recorder is probably the most suitable for the industrial archaeologist. It is not always possible, or even tactful, to suggest connecting up a mains operated tape-recorder when interviewing the 'old inhabitant' in his own home. The portable instrument may be carried round a factory or mill while the purpose of special equipment or the history of some part of the building is explained. Even on the small 3-in reel, a continuous tape record may be taken for well over an hour without breaking the sequence and this is as long as most interviews are likely to last. If longer, the interval for a cup of tea will probably provide an opportunity to turn the tape over for the second instalment.

In recent years the collection of records of the sounds made by vintage locomotives and automobiles has become a cult, but how much better it would be for those enthusiasts to collect and record the reminiscences of the loco drivers or motor mechanics of earlier days who worked on those same engines and cars.

CHAPTER THREE

Maps, Plans and Pictures

A VERY great amount of information is available to the industrial archaeologist in the form of maps, plans and similar topographical material. Before a site is investigated, possibly by excavation, all the available plans should be studied. This gives us a much better idea of what we are looking for, not only saving time and labour at the site, but avoiding the risk of missing important details.

ORDNANCE SURVEY MAPS AND PLANS

Britain has the world's finest Government source of maps and plans, the Ordnance Survey. During the time of the wars with France at the turn of the eighteenth and nineteenth centuries, a need arose for maps for defence purposes, especially in our south-coast areas. The Board of Ordnance, being the most appropriate military body, was directed by Parliament to undertake two main projects: first, to prepare a map of Great Britain to a scale of 1 in to a mile and second, to carry out a trigonometrical survey of England and Wales.

These proposals represented, at the time, a task of considerable magnitude, but it has been far exceeded since those early days; at the present time, the supply of Ordnance Survey maps and plans covers such a wide range that there are few industrial activities which do not, at some time, require them for one purpose or another. Here the latest revision of the maps of the area in question is usually required, but the industrial archaeologist needs to range right back through the various issues and revisions when he is attempting to reconstruct the development of an industrial site.

43

The great range of Ordnance maps is divided for convenience into three classes:

(a) Small scales

(b) Medium scales

(c) Large scales

Classes (a) and (b) are truly maps, as in small and medium scales it is necessary to exaggerate features such as road widths, and to insert conventional signs to indicate features which are unrecognizable at the scale of the map. Class (c) are plans, in which the details are shown to a sufficiently large scale and any distortion becomes unnecessary.

The National Grid is one of the great developments in Ordnance Survey practice arising out of the recommendations of a committee under the chairmanship of Viscount Davidson whose report, published in 1938, had to wait until after the war for its implementation. Before this change of practice, Ordnance maps were based on county areas, each of which had its own meridian. This led to difficulties in fitting maps and plans of adjoining areas. By adopting a different method of projection, the Transverse Mercator, it became possible to select a central meridian from which a system of squares is established based on the international metre. This system of squares known as the National Grid, makes it possible for any point in Great Britain to be given a unique map reference based on its relationship within the Grid to an arbitrarily chosen point which is slightly south-west of the Scilly Isles. No description of a site should lack information of its precise situation based on the National Grid.

Applied as it is throughout the whole country and universally applicable to all scales of maps and plans, the National Grid has led to a new method of subdivision of the sheets of the Ordnance Survey maps themselves. The smaller-scale maps—those habitually carried by almost every motorist, cyclist and walker—thus become the index sheets to the maps and plans of the medium and large scales; so that, by the use of National Grid references, maps may be ordered by post with the certainty that the agent will know exactly what sheets are required.

Small-Scale Maps

This series includes the following:

1. 1/1,125,000 or 1/1¼ million which is based on (3) and is a one-sheet version of it.

2. $\dfrac{1}{M}$ or $\dfrac{1}{1,000,000}$ is to an international scale and includes the National Grid.

3. 1/625,000 or about 10 miles to an inch.

4. ¼ in to a mile, with National Grid.

5. ½ in to a mile. A pre-war series which is at present in abeyance but which is still available in outline and with its original detail unrevised.

6. 1 in to a mile. Probably the best-known Ordnance maps. Now in the Seventh Series. In addition to the coloured sheets, which may be had mounted or unmounted on linen, folded or flat, the 1-in scale is produced in outline for those who wish to add their own additional detail.

Medium-Scale Maps

7. 1/25,000 or approximately 2½ in to a mile.

8. 6 in to a mile.

The first of these is of recent origin following a recommendation of the Davidson Committee that the gap between the 1-in and 6-in maps should be narrowed by a series to an intermediate scale. The 2½-in series was first produced as an expedient during the 1939–45 war by photographic reduction from the 6-in series. It has since been redrawn and while giving much more detail than the 1-in map, it is sufficiently compact to be ideal for walkers. A second series of these maps based on more modern surveys is now being published. The second series covers an area 20 km by 10 km, and the first series covered an area 10 km square.

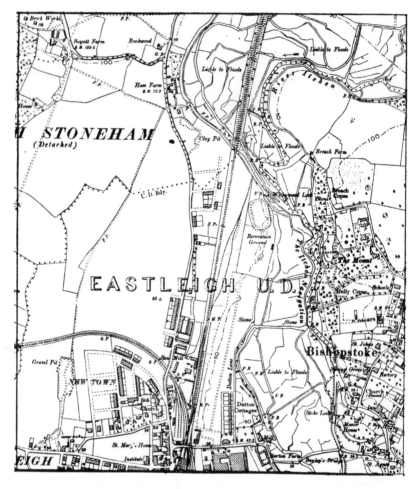

Fig 5. Part of six-inch Ordnance Survey sheet No. LXXIII of 1868 edition, showing state of Eastleigh, a railway town at that time (*printed at a scale of 3.8 in to 1 mile*)

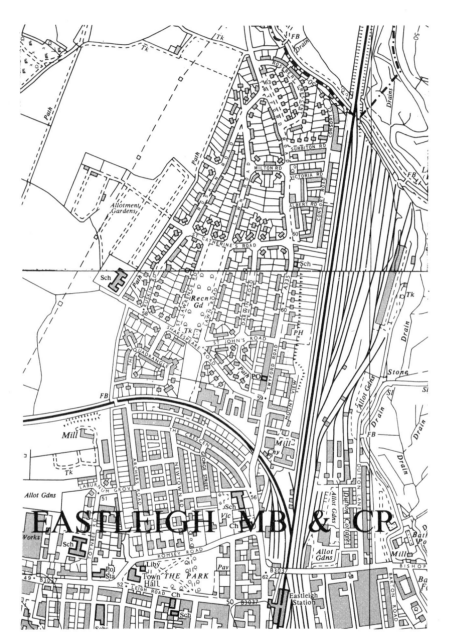

Fig 6. The 1968 edition of the sheet shown in Figure 5, illus-
trating Eastleigh's development (*Crown Copyright reserved*)

The 6-in series is probably the most generally useful for the industrial archaeologist (Figures 5 and 6). It is the largest scale which covers all areas of the country. With the exception of some roads and streets which are shown wider to accommodate street names, it is true-to-scale in its details. It fits into the National Grid pattern with sides scaling 5 k.

Large-Scale Plans

This series covers the following scales:

9. 1/2500 or approximately 25 inches to a mile. The scale known popularly as the '25-in' has been available in the more populated areas for nearly a century. The original sheets were about 38 × 25 in, covering an area of 960 acres. The features on this scale can be shown in considerable detail; for instance, the ordinary gauge of railway track of 4 ft 8½ in is represented by double lines true-to-scale with switches and crossings. The post-war sheets are square, with sides scaling 1 k. (See Figure 7 and Plate 6.)

10. 1/1250, the largest scale now published, being approximately 50 inches to a mile, represents a more detailed series surveyed in town areas only. At this scale, the features of industrial installations such as factories, mills, railways and the like may be shown as true plans. The sheets are published to the same size as the 1/2500, so that each side represents 500 m. (See Figure 8.)

All the maps and plans published since the war are related to the National Grid and all are thus in direct relation one to the other. The whole of Great Britain is divided into squares of 100 km sides, numbered from 00 at the south-west corner to 69 at the north-east. Each of these squares is subdivided into squares of 10 km sides. The resulting squares represent the sheet margins of the 1/25,000 series of maps, the two-figure map reference being the number of the sheet. As the 6-in series is printed on sheets of 5 km sides, each of

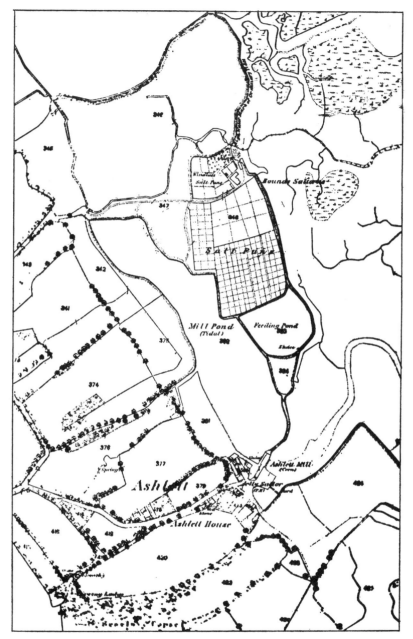

Fig 7. Part of first edition of 1/2500 sheet of Ashlett, near
Fawley, Hampshire, showing the tide mill and its extensive
mill-pond, and also the salterns

PLAN 41/4311 NW

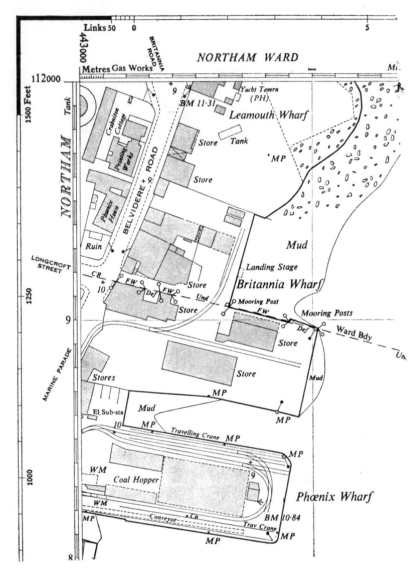

Fig 8. Part of 1/1250 Ordnance sheet 41/4311 covering Itchen Wharves, 1955 edition. Every edition of the maps of this area on the east shore of the Southampton peninsula shows great changes in the pattern of the waterfront (*Crown Copyright reserved*)

the 1/25,000 sheets, if quartered, represents the limits of four of the larger scale, which are described with the map reference of the parent sheet and the compass bearings of the respective sheet corners, ie. NW, NE, SW, SE. The 1/2500 sheets are similarly identified with the four-figure map reference of the 1 km square included in the sheet, while the 1/1250 sheets are quartered in the same way as the 2½- to 6-in relationship.

In addition to the modern series of Ordnance Sheets, the industrial archaeologist will find much of value in the earlier productions of the Ordnance Survey, especially in the larger scales. Many towns had very large-scale plans drawn for special purposes, such as the 60 inches to a mile of London. A very early survey to the same scale is in the possession of the City of Southampton. Still in perfect condition, it was drawn in 1846 by a detachment of the Royal Engineers and represents the highest form of surveying skill. Plans to this scale were first authorized in 1840 for towns in the north of England and, about ten years later, authority was given for a special series of town plans to a scale of 1/528 or 10 ft to a mile. Most of these plans were made following the Public Health Act of 1848 and the *First Report of the Commissioners for Inquiring into the State of Large Towns and Populous Districts* which was published in 1844. They were surveyed at the expense of the towns concerned and, in many cases, were acquired by the civic authorities in the original manuscript form. Such plans may be most valuable to the industrial archaeologist as, being in such detail and so meticulously accurate, they may often become a starting point of his topographical researches. A later period, the 1870s and 1880s, brought a fine series of town plans published by the OS to a scale of 1/500.

Many of the features shown on Ordnance maps, both the modern and earlier editions, represent relics of activities of the past which, if not investigated quickly, will be permanently lost to future historians. An example of this may be demonstrated by the rapid industrial development of the New Forest shore of Southampton

Water on which, since 1950, two large power stations, a major oil company with its associated industries, and other smaller installations have been sited. A half-century ago and earlier, the principal means of communication to the hamlets and farms adjoining this coast was by ship, but the foreshore consists of alluvial mud which extended a long distance to the main shipping channel (Figure 9). It was therefore necessary to make and maintain small access channels to the farms and private estates along that shore. This was achieved by the process of sluicing: a large volume of water was impounded at high tide, and at low tide this was used to scour a channel by the shortest route to deep water. Early editions of the Ordnance Survey show the existence of a number of such sluiced channels and their associated basins. The artificial channels, as might be expected, are easily identified by their straightness, and from a study of the Ordnance Sheet it can be seen that the cost of embanking an artificial scouring basin was reduced or avoided by making use of natural features when possible. In the twenty years since the war, reclamation of the foreshore has progressively covered all these creeks and their scouring basins, leaving no evidence of their existence except for the maps, and such photographs as it was possible to take before their demise.

GEOLOGICAL MAPS

This special kind of map may be of great use to the student of many branches of industrial archaeology, especially those connected with the mineral industries. The incidence of building materials is also closely associated with the geology of a district, while those engaged in the design and execution of many engineering works such as water supply, tunnels and canals require a good knowledge of local geology if they are to keep out of trouble and choose the easiest routes.

Geological maps show, as far as careful field work will allow, the

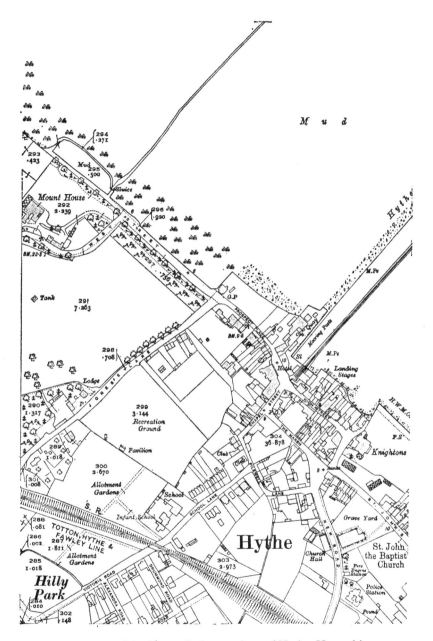

Fig 9. Part of the 1/2500 Ordnance sheet of Hythe, Hampshire, 1932 edition, showing the sluicing basins and the channels sluiced through the mud (*Crown Copyright reserved*)

outcrop below the soil and superficial deposits of geological forma-
tions. Given the deviation from the horizontal of each layer (the
dip) and the direction of a horizontal line on the stratum (the strike),
it is possible to assess the local tendency of the layer. As nature
rarely, if ever, behaves in a textbook manner, the problem is complicated by the effects of earth movements in the past which have
led to irregularities such as faults. It is possible, however, to pack a
large amount of information on to the two-dimensional sheet of a
geological map which may be interpreted by a skilful reader in
terms of the three-dimensional structure underground.

The coloured geological maps of the British Isles are produced by
a department organized for the purpose, the Geological Survey. The
general map of the Survey, to a scale of 25 miles to an inch, gives a
good picture of the geological structure of the country as a whole,
especially for matters such as the distribution of minerals, or
building materials. For the worker requiring more detail, the ¼-in
maps in twenty-three sheets covering England and Wales, or the
1-in maps, are available according to need. The Old Series of 1-in
Geological Maps, commenced more than a century ago, has now
been almost entirely superseded by the New Series, which although
it does not cover all areas, may be found to embrace every district
in which minerals are of economic importance.

In addition to its maps, the Geological Survey publishes memoirs
of the areas covered by many of the maps and also a series of
Regional Handbooks which are most valuable as supplements to the
information shown on the maps.

DIRECTORY MAPS

Some of the early directories and guide-books contained maps of
the district which were produced from the work of local surveyors.
Although the quality of these will vary according to the competence
(and perhaps the conscience) of the surveyor, they will probably in-

clude worthwhile information for the industrial archaeologist. Plate 2 is a good example of this kind of map: showing the Borough of Reading in 1813, it includes in its details the locks leading from the Thames to the Kennet Navigation and also the mills using that head of water which made the locks necessary.

Sometimes a local surveyor produced maps for general sale. Such a man would be engaged in a professional capacity by the commissioners of the various public activities in his neighbourhood, and would find ultimately that he had surveyed the whole of a district for one client or another. His surveys could then be re-plotted to one scale for the engraver to produce a copper plate. Prints from the plate would command a ready sale in plain or coloured versions.

RAILWAY MAPS AND PLANS

The railways of Britain, in the course of a century and a quarter, have produced maps and plans in great numbers, ranging from maps printed for inclusion in timetables to large-scale plans showing the layout and details of stations, dock lines or shunting yards. The major railway companies maintained up-to-date plans of their property on a scale appropriate to the amount of detail to be shown. Those on the Great Western were, for instance, 2 chains to an inch for the standard survey of the line, with larger-scale plans at 40 ft to an inch where required. The use of plans of 2 chains to an inch eased the task of measuring land areas, a very important factor on plans showing every piece of acquired land separately. As 10 square chains equal 1 acre, an area on the plan of $2\frac{1}{2}$ square in equals 1 acre at this scale, so that the number of square inches on the plan multiplied by 2/5 gives the number of acres of land. Equally conveniently, as 80 chains equal 1 mile, 10 in on the plan equals $\frac{1}{4}$ mile or 20 chains.

Larger scales have been used for the more important railway installations, such as stations, goods yards, railway-owned docks and wharves, 40 ft to an inch being quite a usual scale and on this a considerable amount of detail may be shown. As the railways form such an intimate part of the community, these plans can rarely stop strictly at the property boundary, especially in such areas as docks. They may therefore show detail which may not be available from other sources, especially when the problem is one of dating buildings or other features.

TITHE MAPS

The Ordnance Survey, with its 1/500, 1/528 and larger-scale plans of towns, covered urban areas fairly adequately from the 1840s onward. There was, however, another series of maps produced about that time which, while giving some attention to the towns, provides a great deal of valuable topographical information about the rural areas. These are the tithe maps, made to meet the requirements of the Tithe Commutation Act of 1836 which was designed to change the payment in kind of tithes on land to a settlement in money. For the necessary assessment of values, an accurate survey was made of thousands of parishes and three copies of each map and award were made for the parish, the diocesan records and the central records.

For the first time since Domesday Book was prepared, the countryside was subjected to a detailed scrutiny. The areas surveyed included on the tithe map such information as the ownership and occupation of every piece of land, the names of farms, mills, fields and other uses of the land in full detail. In most cases, the parish copy is still available, and if not the diocesan; failing either, the Tithe Redemption Commission, Finsbury Square, EC4, is still in possession of a copy of every tithe map prepared according to the Act.

ENCLOSURE MAPS

The 1836 Act did not apply to lands of which the tithes had

already been extinguished as part of the provisions of an earlier enclosure Act. In these, the tithe was converted into an equivalent allocation of land and dealt with accordingly. The period of greatest activity in the enclosure of land was during the second half of the eighteenth century, when millions of acres of open field were enclosed by authority of private Acts of Parliament. The maps associated with these activities offer much topographical information covering a period immediately before the explosive growth of industry in the early nineteenth century. Enclosure maps are usually available at the county record offices—some have them catalogued; while in other cases the local historical society possesses a list published in its *Proceedings*, based on the work of Dr W. E. Tate.

The enclosure of land, whether from open field or from common lands, is important to the industrial archaeologist who is interested in the road pattern of his area. One of the consequences of enclosure was the extinction of many ancient roads or rights-of-way and their replacement by new roads, mostly outside the area enclosed. In many rural areas the motorist who is following an apparently devious route may be using a road built originally in the late eighteenth century around an enclosure of land.

PROPERTY PLANS

The plans prepared by estate agents in connection with sales of property may usefully reveal industrial topography. They may show a planned layout which was never completed and thus explain the reason for an unorthodox layout. The Polygon area in Southampton is such a case: the intention of promoters at the close of the eighteenth century was to build an estate of houses for upper-middle-class owners, in the shape of a polygon, and the town maps of that period show the proposed final layout. The scheme went no further than the first couple of houses and the present awkwardly sited Polygon Hotel is all that is left.

Plans attached to legal documents such as leases or conveyances of property can be most valuable in establishing such facts as the date of building or the sequence of construction. Sometimes a building may be considerably extended, often by more than its original size, but in a style and with materials in accord with the original structure; the plans on legal documents may be the only evidence of the two stages of construction. The plan shown as Figure 10 is just such a document, showing why a particular warehouse has five storeys at one end (plus a cellar) and six storeys at

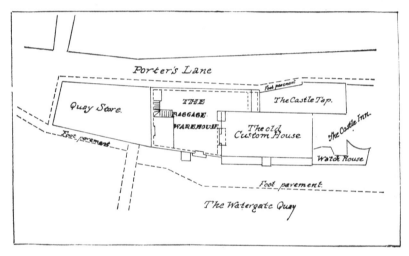

Fig 10. Tracing from Assignment of Lease, showing Baggage
Warehouse now incorporated in later warehouse

the other. This plan is one attached to the Assignment of a Lease of the Baggage Warehouse dated 1850 from the Secretary of the Customs to the Commissioners of the Port & Harbour of Southampton. The document, like many others of its kind, gives the previous history of the site:

the scite of ground whereon certain premises called the Woolhouse formerly stood being on the North side of the Town Wall immediately at the back of the said Custom House bounded with the stone stairs on the East with a lane called Porters Lane on the North and with a storehouse belonging to the Commissioners for Improving the Port of the Town of Southampton erected on a void piece of ground late other part of the said Woolhouse on the West.

In 1866, the Commissioners built an extension on the Baggage Warehouse, and the structure as it stands today may be seen in Plate 4, from which the two storeys of the earlier building may be identified. Not only is this building still in use, but the Custom House is occupied as offices. The Castle Inn of 1850 was originally a part of the Water Gate of the fourteenth-century town wall and has now been restored. The small building shown as a Watch House is now gone, but was used in the earlier years of this century to house a rotary electrical transformer—also gone. This typical plan shows how much local industrial history may be gleaned from one legal document.

OLD ENGRAVINGS, DRAWINGS AND PAINTINGS

The spread to the middle classes of the habit of a fortnight's summer holiday encouraged the publication of books of views of the favoured district. These may still be found in second-hand bookshops, although they tend to be broken up for the engravings to be framed and sold at much higher prices. In many of the early books the copper or steel engravings were taken from drawings of good topographical artists and can provide valuable information. Due allowance must be made for artists' licence as, although some were extremely accurate in their delineation, others appear to have made very rough sketches at the site, finishing the drawing in the studio.

The value of such engravings taken in conjunction with other material is shown by Plate 3, one of the engravings by Philip Brannon, a Southampton artist and architect of the mid-nineteenth century who published a series of books of views. The author also

possesses a manuscript letter from John Doswell Doswell, an eminent engineer and surveyor, who practised in Southampton for the
first half of the same century; the letter was to the chairman of one of
Doswell's many public-authority clients and recommends the provision of timber fendering on a sea wall recently completed to proposals of John Rennie, the famous engineer. These two documents,
separated by about thirty years, show the original scheme and the
manner of its final execution.

   The Brannon engraving includes a number of buildings which
were still in existence before the 1940 air-raids on Southampton,
and some of which remain. All are of interest to the industrial
archaeologist. The central feature is the Royal Southern Yacht Club
building, opened in 1843 and virtually unaltered today, although it
has been used for other purposes for over a quarter century. The
building with a pitched tiled roof is the Wool House, a fourteenth-
century warehouse for wool brought by packhorse from a wide
hinterland for shipping to the Continent; it is now beautifully
restored for use as a maritime museum. Every industrial archaeologist who can should visit it to see the roof framing of Spanish
chestnut and oak. Right again is the Royal Victoria Pier Hotel, contemporary with the pier (*circa* 1835) and—also bombed in 1940—
one of an interesting range of warehouses built on the foundations
of the old town walls. Comparison with the known features on the
ground show that this engraving is reliable, although Brannon was
not always as accurate as this.

   Before the days of the photograph, the artist and engraver provided illustrative material to satisfy the demands of books, newspapers, the parlour walls and all the other uses. The great topographical artists, such as Turner, Paul Sandby, Samuel Prout, as
well as local artists, prepared sets of drawings for engraving and
publishing as books of views. Turner's *Ports and Harbours of
Britain* engraved by Finden, is an example. Notepaper printed with
a local view as a heading was fashionable in mid-Victorian times.

Many of the weekly and monthly periodicals found that woodcuts increased their interest and sales; the *Illustrated London News* was probably the most successful example, although less pretentious journals such as the *Penny Magazine* and the *Mechanic's Magazine* included illustrations of great interest to the industrial archaeologist. Figures 11, 12 and 13 are examples from such sources.

Fig 11. Illustration from *Penny Magazine* of 16 July 1836

In spite of a demand for old prints created by tourism and by the fashion for hotels and public-houses to decorate their walls with them, there are still many thousands available in the bookshops and print shops throughout the country. Most of the prints of value to the industrial archaeologist are not those on display, with Hogarth frames and high prices; they lie in the basement or back room in

Fig 12. Engraving of the Sunderland iron bridge, from the *European Magazine* of 1 July 1796

portfolios or even brown paper parcels, and their examination will probably require some mutual understanding and patience on the part of both buyer and seller. It will also require some tolerance to dust in the nostrils and on the fingers.

Local and central collections which may be explored for such illustrative material include not only the great London and provincial museums, art galleries and libraries, but often those in the

ITCHEN FERRY

Fig 13. Illustration from the *Graphic* of 14 July 1883, showing
the chain ferry or floating bridge across the Itchen

smaller towns. A local library or museum often has the custody of
one or more collections of prints, drawings, or papers left by some
enthusiast long since gone. Some of these in themselves can be the
starting point of more than one research project into the industrial
or social history of a community. The custodian may be a university,
as in the case of the Brunel sketchbooks and notebooks, which have
been passed to the library of the University of Bristol by Lady
Noble.

An old print drawn and engraved by accurate artists may provide
valuable technical evidence as in the case of the engraving reproduced as Plate 1. An engineer experienced in the processes illustrated
in this picture of the demolition of Old London Bridge will appre-

ciate the accuracy of all the details. The piles being drawn from the
river-bed were probably driven at the time the bridge was first built
by Peter of Colechurch in the fourteenth century. Plate 10 is of a
part of one of a number of piles recovered at Southampton in 1949
on the probable site of the Woolbridge, a jetty built in the same
century. A number of these piles were very similar to those being
drawn from London Bridge, which strengthens the view that they
were of the same period.

Another interesting comparison may be made between Plates 11
and 12. These represent cranes of the early nineteenth century; that
in Plate 11 is at Burbage Wharf on the Kennet & Avon Canal; it is
dated 1832 on the iron band at the top of the centre post. Although
these cranes are different in design, the materials and workmanship
are both typical of the millwright's craft of the time.

By the fourth quarter of the nineteenth century, photography had
reached such a standard of excellence that it was in frequent use
for recording events and objects in the industrial world. As in the
case of other records, old collections of photographs are occasionally
discovered in the most unexpected places. The author had the
pleasure, a few years ago, of being able to pass on to the proper
custodians a collection of about 350 beautiful photographs of the
Southampton, Salisbury and Winchester areas. These had been
taken by a local professional for the publishers of a series of guide-
books and were saved from destruction by a narrow margin of good
fortune. Plate 5 is reproduced from one of these photographs,
which is as good as anything that a modern photographer can produce with all his technical advantages.

Picture postcards are to be found in most second-hand bookshops
and similar places. The tendency in postcard presentation of local
topography was almost always to photograph the park and not the
gasworks, but among the vast numbers published, a goodly proportion illustrate the condition of the main street of the town and such
buildings as the railway station, town hall and other monuments of

Plate 1. Demolition of Old London Bridge, showing the same kind of rough-hewn piles as those found at Southampton in 1949 (shown in Plate 10)

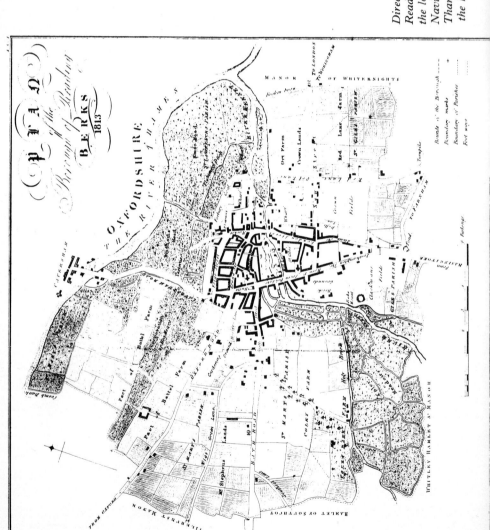

Plate 2.

Directory or guide-book map of Reading. Dated 1813, it shows the locks connecting the Kennet Navigation with the River Thames, and also the mills using the head of water at the locks

Victorian prosperity. Ships and locomotives were also popular subjects for postcard art.

Hilaire Belloc wrote that 'rich men like small windfalls' and often the small gift of a letter, sketch, print or photograph will please the collector of historical material because of its relevance to his immediate studies. It therefore follows that the industrial archaeologist should not keep his interest in the subject a secret. An occasional letter to the local press when a topographical or biographical problem is under discussion, or perhaps a short article of local interest, will sometimes bring contacts and correspondence of great value. The author has many documents of interest which have come by such means, sometimes from anonymous donors.

E

CHAPTER FOUR

Surveying

THE archaeologist who is investigating a prehistoric or Roman site has no contemporary plans on which to work. The industrial archaeologist, however, usually has the advantage of some written or drawn information from one of the sources referred to in the previous chapters. So valuable is such material, that the effort and time taken to trace it will usually be well repaid when proceeding further, but, nevertheless, it will usually be necessary to survey any site being opened up or building being investigated.

If this is being done by a group, it is possible that one or more members of the group will have had some previous experience of surveying and levelling, in which case his skill will, no doubt, be utilized. But the independent investigator, or the group without an expert, can by the application of a modest combination of elementary geometry and common sense produce a competent plan of a site extending over a few acres. Such a plan can be sufficiently accurate to supplement the details of the Ordnance Survey and to illustrate a report or an article for the press.

The professional surveyor has at his disposal a number of items of expensive equipment which are necessary if he is to survey large areas to a considerable degree of accuracy. He is also, as a rule, under pressure to produce his results in a minimum of time. The industrial archaeologist may take a little longer, but should not feel discouraged by the simplicity of his gear.

EQUIPMENT REQUIRED FOR A SIMPLE SURVEY

The Chain

The surveyor's chain, introduced by Edmund Gunter in the

66

seventeenth century, is 66 ft long and consists of 100 links; each link is the same length of 7·92 in, or 66/100 ft. The length of 66 ft, or 22 yd, is convenient to the surveyor, much of whose work involves the measurement of land areas in acres. Ten square chains or 22 yd by 220 yd equal 4,840 square yd, which is an acre, and the principal unit in land measurement.

For many modern needs, however, chains of 100 ft long are more convenient, and these are also used widely, especially in railway, dock and industrial work. Figure 14 shows a folded chain.

Whether a chain is 66 or 100 ft long, each link or unit of measurement consists of one long and three short links, totalling 7·92 or 12 in respectively. The end links have a swivelling handle of brass for convenience, the handle being included in the unit length so that the whole chain, with handles, is true to its nominal length. A surveyor's chain may be used from either end, so it is provided at every tenth link with a brass tag, or teller, of the form shown in Figure 15. These are symmetrical about the central 50 tag.

A surveyor's chain is a very robust piece of equipment and remains reasonably accurate under rough handling. It is, however, necessary to prove its accuracy at intervals, preferably once a day before starting work. This may be done by stretching it between two carefully measured points, which may be nails driven into a tarmac or asphalt surface, such as a footpath, or chisel marks on a suitable flat concrete area. If the chain has stretched it may be adjusted by using a hammer to shorten the short links slightly, distributing this adjustment throughout the chain.

The folding of a chain after use, if not done by the proper method, can lead to a tangle which is difficult to unravel. The chain may be folded from one end, or from the centre, the latter being the quicker. On finishing work, the handles should be brought together by drawing one back to the other, leaving 50 ft or links of double chain lying in a straight line with the handles together. The pair of links adjoining the 50 mark are then picked up in the left hand, while the right hand picks up the next pair but one, laying these across the pair in the left hand at a slight angle. This process is repeated until the whole chain is picked up and folded, the assembly then looking like a corn stook with the short links at each end of the bundle and the handles outside. The expert surveyor can reverse this process by holding both handles in the left hand and throwing the remainder of the chain forward, but a novice may find it better to grasp both handles, drop the chain and drag it forward, unravelling itself as it goes.

The chain may be dispensed with if two measuring tapes are available, by using a string line for maintaining the alignment of the survey lines. A good length of builders' line is suitable for this purpose, although a length of any good string will serve at a pinch. It should be long enough to extend the full length of the longest line of the survey, or up to 500 ft, whichever is the longest; longer lines may be string lined by extending the alignment with ranging rods.

Measuring Tapes

It is possible to carry out a chain survey without any other measuring equipment than a chain and a measuring rod, but it would be very inconvenient. Measuring tapes in one form or another are an important part of every surveyor's outfit today. An engineer, whose survey may be required for the manufacture of a complicated layout of railway switch and crossing work, will use a steel measuring band instead of the Gunter chain. His line, set out precisely with a theodolite, will probably be maintained by a tensioned string line between nails driven into pegs at short intervals, and from this he will measure his offsets with another steel tape. From his survey, plotted to a scale of 8 ft or perhaps even 4 ft to an inch, it will be possible to manufacture a layout which will fit without trouble into an existing system of points and crossings. If the new installation has to be put in over a period of a few hours on a wet night, the importance of a precise survey may be appreciated.

Although the industrial archaeologist is not likely to need a steel band, he may frequently find the string line technique useful for use with linen tapes which are, in any case, much more convenient to handle and transport than the chain. The usual range of linen tapes available in this country are 100 ft, 66 ft, 50 ft and 33 ft. These may be had reinforced with metal wire to reduce the risk of the tape stretching. All are made up in circular leather or plastic cases with folding metal winders and a suitable selection for measuring industrial sites or plant would be one each of 100 ft and 50 ft, the 100 ft for main 'chain' lines and the 50 ft for offsets. A 6 ft measuring rod, either of the architect's folding type or of the convex self-supporting steel section, will be useful for measuring details.

Markers

Every surveyor requires a good supply of marking devices. These fall into two categories (a) ranging rods and (b) arrows. Ranging rods are usually of wood, with pointed steel shoes. They are about 1 in diameter or a little more, and are painted at 1-ft intervals in alternate red, black and white. Not only do the markings make the rods more visible, but the 1 ft interval is useful as an approximate measurement for indeterminate features such as hedgerows. The steel-shod end of the rod is also useful for extending the ring of a measuring tape to a point otherwise inaccessible.

Arrows are skewer-shaped pins made of steel wire about 3/16 in diameter and normally 15 in long, although 18- and 24-in lengths are available. They have a bent eye at one end, about $1\frac{1}{2}$ in diameter, and are pointed at the other (Figure 16). Their main purpose is to mark the end of each chain or 100 ft of a chain survey, although being very light and portable, they are often used for marking temporarily any point in a survey for which a ranging rod may not be available. If an arrow is used for this purpose, a piece of paper or rag impaled on it will make it easier to find.

Wooden pegs about 2 in square and 2 ft long, pointed at one end

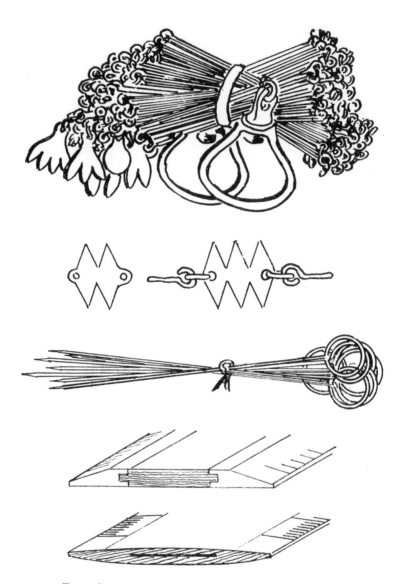

Top to bottom:
Fig 14. Survey chain folded for carrying
Fig 15. Alternative pattern of tellers for survey chain
Fig 16. Surveyor's arrows
Fig 17. Two patterns of scales

for easier driving, are very useful on any survey and essential on some. A suitable hammer will of course be required for driving them. If pegs are being used in connection with a string line survey, some 2-in or 2½-in wire nails will be required. One of these will be driven into the top of a peg wherever it is necessary to secure the line.

Field Book

The surveyor's field book is usually 6 in by 4 in or 8 in by 4 in and is bound to open on the short edge. It should have good waterproof pages and a strong cover with a pencil pocket. The Ordnance Survey had a rule for many years that all bookings should be in ink and field workers carried a portable ink bottle for the purpose. Nowadays, the ubiquitous ball pen, preferably a black one, serves the same purposes more conveniently. Pencil notes may become indecipherable if put down in rainy weather, or in an industrial atmosphere with coal dust or some other pollutant falling around. The book is provided with one or two lines down the page which represent the survey line. Bookings are made from bottom to top, as measurements progress along the line.

Plotting Equipment

Plotting must always be done on good quality paper, the cost of which is trivial in comparison with the time spent. Paper expands and contracts with changes of weather and this is an important matter when the plan is to be scaled to a great degree of accuracy. Metal plates are often used for professional work when stability of shape and size are important, but for the industrial archaeologist a 'hot pressed' paper of good make will be adequate. Cartridge paper will do for many purposes and may be obtained in sheets or as a roll.

Surveys are usually plotted on a horizontal surface which, for large plans, consists of a plotting table of adequate size. A thick plywood drawing board of sufficient size to take a sheet of paper for plotting the plan to a suitable scale will suffice for most purposes likely to be met by the industrial archaeologist. To this the paper may be secured by drawing pins, clips, or adhesive tape. A straight edge roughly equal to the diagonal of the board and a pair of pencil compasses will also be necessary.

Scales may vary in style and quality from cheap cardboard sets to those engraved on ivory. Between these two extremes, they may be found made of wood—boxwood is usual—of celluloid or plastic, alone or reinforced with boxwood or metal, or of metal alone. It is doubtful if ivory scales are obtainable today except by special order at great expense, but at one time, say before 1914, it was the ambition of every good draughtsman to own a set. They may still be found in second-hand shops, and if in reasonable condition are worth acquiring, if only as an investment. The scales more likely to be used for survey work will be of white plastic, reinforced with metal, or combined with a boxwood centre. They are supplied in 'oval' or 'flat' sections, as shown in Figure 17, and may be divided in many ways, most of which will serve at a pinch for plotting. The ideal scale for survey plotting is of the flat section, with white edges divided in black; it should be divided with the scale required on both edges with what are described as full divisions—that is, divided along its whole length in the same manner. For instance, a scale of twentieths will have inches divided into twenty parts along its whole length, starting from zero at the same end on both edges. The surveyor may thus plot his line from either edge as convenient.

Offsets may be plotted more conveniently with the use of an offset scale. These are usually about 2 in long and the best for general use are divided in both directions from the centre. Again, it is best to use the same division on both edges; mistakes can happen and to use a wrong scale on, say, a 30/40 divided scale may lead to serious errors in the plot.

After the survey is plotted, it should be inked in, using waterproof black drawing ink in a draughtsman's drawing pen. The drawing pen will be, to some extent, a matter of choice; it will be convenient to have two, one with the nibs rather narrow, for drawing in the details of a small scale survey, and one with broad nibs for drawing thicker lines such as borders. The broader nibs hold more ink and care must be used to avoid blotting the survey by opening them too wide. The narrow nib pen should not be so fine as to lead to difficulty in maintaining line thickness; expert draughtsmen may use a lithographic drawing pen, which is favoured by professional cartographers but has extremely thin nibs and is liable, in the hands of the inexpert, to close completely, leaving no line at all. The nibs of the drawing pen must be sharp and must be absolutely equal in length. This may be tested by drawing a ghost line on a piece of tracing paper with an empty pen with the nibs open about 1/32 in. If the pressure is light and the pen held absolutely upright, a difference of a thousandth of an inch will be evident.

All surveys, with the exception of air surveys, depend on the measurement of lengths and angles on the ground, the systematic booking of this information in relation to the objects to be recorded, and the translation by plotting of the same information to a chosen scale on paper or other suitable medium. With the exception of the simplest form of survey, based on a single line, as perhaps of a village street frontage, a survey is developed on a skeleton of lines. Measured on the ground, these are reconstructed on paper to a chosen scale and from them the details are similarly measured and plotted. For this purpose we use that stable and reproducible geometrical figure, the triangle, as an essential part of the technique of surveying.

To construct any triangle we need as a minimum (a) the length of all three sides; (b) of the two sides and one angle; or (c) one side and two angles. If, therefore, it is possible to measure all three sides, a triangle may be plotted to any scale. As it is usually possible to reproduce these conditions on the kind of site likely to be encountered by the industrial archaeologist, or to create them by designing the system of survey lines, the use of an angle-measuring instrument at the site may be avoided.

If the site is an open one, it is best to build up a skeleton of survey lines as a system of triangles, as in Figure 18. Many industrial sites,

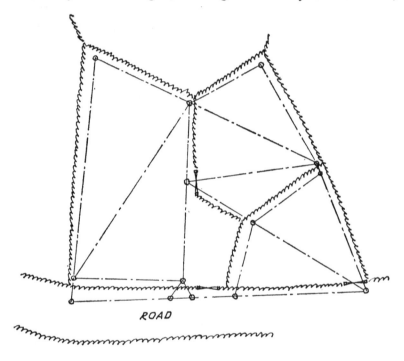

ROAD

Fig 18. Triangulation of a field

however, abound in obstructions and it may be necessary to resort to a traverse. This is a system of lines connected by measured intersecting angles, as in Figure 19 which indicates how the angles of intersection may be measured by extending each survey line and measuring a tie line to establish the angle. This is an open traverse

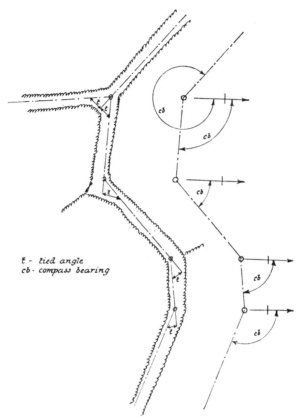

Fig 19. Traverse of a road

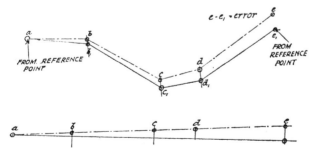

Fig 20. Method of correcting traverse

and is not self-checking, but such a traverse may be checked by plotting the lines to an appropriate Ordnance Survey plan. This is done by the professional surveyor who uses what are known as Reference Points on the Ordnance plans; these are features in the landscape likely to be permanent, such as corners of buildings, bridge abutments, etc, which are marked on modern editions of the large-scale Ordnance plans by the letters *rp*.

The best way of proving a traverse is to close it, or to continue the survey lines in a circuit and return to starting point when, in theory, the end of the last line should coincide with the beginning of the first. In practice this never happens unless the inevitable errors of measurement cancel each other out. As a rule, there is a small error which is disclosed in the plotted result and which is proportioned out between the survey lines by an accepted method which is shown in Figure 20.

A PRACTICAL EXAMPLE

Many of the procedures adopted in a simple survey of an industrial site may be better understood by the novice if described against the background of a practical example. The one chosen is based on a survey made by the author many years ago at a port then engaged mostly in shipping coal for export. The installation surveyed was reconstructed shortly afterward; in fact the survey was for the purpose of planning the new layout. Subsequent changes in the economic pattern of the area have led to the demolition of the later installation, and the survey thus forms the only record of a small bit of the extensive coal-shipping equipment in a port which had its coaling heyday at the beginning of this century, and has now almost entirely changed its function.

The area surveyed includes the railways leading to a coaling jetty and hoist. There are turntables, weighbridges, switches and crossings and hauling equipment for pulling the trucks. The hoist, on reinforced concrete stanchions, is supported on a jetty at the dock-side, the water level of which is approximately constant.

The whole survey was possible without a theodolite, the triangulation being schemed out to avoid obstacles while allowing short offsets from the survey lines to most important points, those of greatest importance being 'tied in'. A steel band measure of 100 ft length was used for the main survey lines, as the plotting was to be to a scale of 1/96, or 8 ft to an inch, for the purpose of designing the new installation. For an industrial record, a scale of 20 ft to an inch would probably be appropriate, and for this an ordinary surveyor's chain or even a linen tape would be accurate enough. With this difference, the procedures and equipment could be the same.

A walk around the site with a few ranging rods determines the position of the main survey lines. The end of each is, in the first instance, marked with a ranging rod, those starting from another line being carefully lined up. All lines must be checked to ensure that the chain or tape may be laid straight and fairly level along its whole length. On a small survey such as this, there is no real need for a check chaining, but the novice may find it convenient to measure the length of his lines and plot them to a small scale to check that he has allowed for a complete triangulation. On a large survey, say for a large factory, railway or dock installation, where the surveyor's home base may be many miles away, it is a prudent rule to check the pattern of lines as they are chained, so that a field check by re-chaining or observing the angles may be made while the survey party is at the site. For a large survey, this may mean some improvisation and it has been known for check plots to be made with the hotel bedroom floor as the plotting table.

As the pattern of survey lines is the most important part of a survey, it takes pride of place in the survey book. Thus Figure 21 shows the first page of the bookings of our practical example. The sketch need not be to scale, but if the pattern tends to be complicated, then an approximation to scale will be desirable. It may

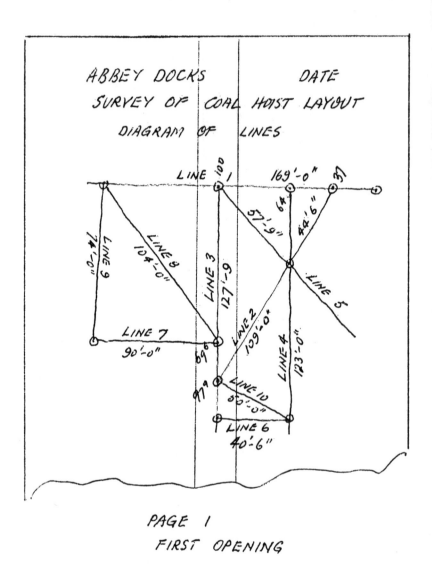

PAGE 1

FIRST OPENING

Fig 21. Diagram of lines for survey, page 1 of field book

appear that some of the lines are redundant, but a study of the completed plot will show that each line is necessary to establish the full data for the triangulation, that it enables the surveyor to keep the length of his offsets short or that it picks up details which would not be easily measured from lines of the main triangulation.

If the survey is a small one and may be completed in a day, there is probably no need to drive pegs as a record of the key points in the system. If, however, any of the ranging rods is liable to be knocked out of position or removed, it may be necessary either to drive a peg or, alternatively, to record its position in relation to the nearest fixed objects. A sketch in the field book giving its position and the necessary measurements will enable the end of an important line, or the junction of several, to be established at any time. As already mentioned, the Ordnance Survey recognizes the need for such a relocation of position by the establishing of reference points on the most recent editions of the large scale plans. The co-ordinates of all these points are recorded in reference to the National Grid and any subsequent survey work may be fitted to the Ordnance Sheets. The lists of reference points for any area may be obtained from the same sources as the Ordnance maps and plans themselves.

Procedure for the actual chaining depends on whether the surveyor has one chainman or two. If the latter, which is preferable, he may devote all his attention to his booking and to the overall supervision of his survey. If he has one chainman only, he must then act as following chainman, thus slowing the work, increasing the chance of error and, by getting his hands dirty, making his survey book dirtier than necessary. We may assume that the industrial archaeologist who is carrying out a small survey will have two able-bodied volunteers to help as chainmen and describe the procedure accordingly. The chain (or tape) for the chaining being laid out in the approximate direction of the first line, the leading chainman will line it up under the direction of the following chainman. Both are provided with ranging rods, the leading man holding his rod and the chain handle while straining the chain, moving it laterally to the instructions of the following chainman, who lines up the ranging rod of the leading man with the rod at the end of the survey line. He is simultaneously holding the trailing end of the chain (or tape) in position. This is harder to describe than to do, but the object is simply to have the chain in a straight line on the ground pointing dead in the direction of the ranging rod marking the end of the line.

Having done this, the leading chainman, who is carrying ten arrows at the beginning of the line, pushes one into the ground at the first 100 ft mark and, leaving the chain on the ground, joins his fellow chainman to measure offsets. These are booked by the surveyor in his field book, starting at the bottom of the page and working upward as he progresses along the line. Assuming he has a field book with double lines, he books his chainage between the lines, his left and right offsets on the appropriate sides of the book. It is not usual to draw every object in detail in the field book: symbols are used which are often developed by experience in any industry. These symbols are a kind of shorthand and, as with shorthand, the symbols recognized generally are more useful than those invented by an individual. It should ideally be possible for any experienced surveyor to plot the survey from any field book.

It is usual to note the end of a survey line by the symbol of a dot in a circle. This applies to the end of lines which are picked up when chaining along any line; our first line starts therefore with this symbol.

Pages 81 to 84 show the field book notes of the survey now being described. The chainmen, having aligned the chain, take the linen tape for measuring the offsets and tie measurements. The leading chainman carries the ring end of the tape and also a ranging rod. While he places the ring extremity of the tape at the point to be measured, his following chainman squares off the tape over the chain and calls out the chainage first, then the offset measurement. He gauges the squareness of his tape by eye; if the offset is short,

Plate 3. *Engraving by Philip Brannon of sea wall and buildings at Southampton Pier, circa 1845*

Plate 4. *Warehouse at Southampton, built 1866, incorporating an earlier Customs baggage warehouse of late eighteenth century*

Plate 5. Foreshore at Southampton, about 1895. The walls still exist, but successive reclamations of land from the sea have altered the scene

Plate 6. Ashlett tide mill, near Fawley, now a club house for Esso Sports & Social Club

say up to 20 ft, any error in squareness will be less than the tolerable error. If an object is a considerable distance from the chain and its position is important, then it should be 'tied in', as shown on the field book entries. The bookings of line 1 of our survey show a number of important points tied in (Figures 22 and 23), such as the corners of the coal bin, the turntables, the weighbridge and the weighbridge office. The offsets to the railway track are measured to

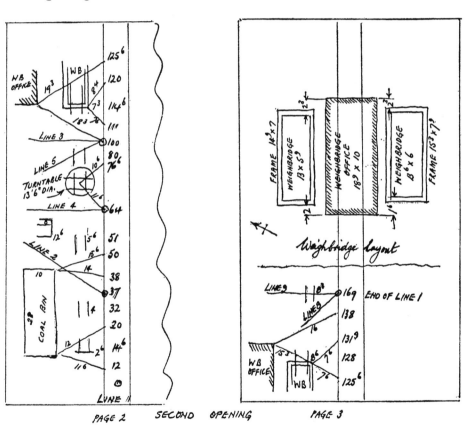

PAGE 2   SECOND OPENING   PAGE 3

Figs 22 and 23. Pages 2 and 3 of field book notes

F

the running face of the nearest rail; no measurement being booked to the farther rail although it is indicated. The railway gauge of 4 ft 8½ in is assumed unless otherwise indicated. A crossing is always indicated by an X and, for small scales, may be measured at the nose of the crossing, although the actual position of inter-section may be a few inches away. The thickness of the crossing nose must be taken into account for accurate large-scale plans.

Where complicated detail would make the field book difficult to follow, it is usual to supplement the bookings with a sketch. The weighbridge layout is a good example of this as it demonstrates also the risk of assuming symmetry in a layout. In this case, two weigh-bridges were installed, possibly at different dates, the dimensions differing to an extent that would be material on a large-scale plan.

As the chainmen work along the line, they reach the first 100, where the arrow marks the actual 100 ft distance. The leading chain-man then pulls the chain forward by its handle to the next 100, which the following chainman will indicate when the trailing end reaches the arrow. The aligning procedure is then repeated, the leading chainman putting in a second arrow, the following chainman picking up the first. By this device, the surveyor will always know the chainage by the number of arrows carried by the following chainman, who accompanies him through the survey. Any doubt of the accuracy may be checked by the leading chainman's arrows, which, with the one at the end of chain, should make a total of ten.

Line 2 of our example shows the line crossing a number of features diagonally and indicates how crossing points are booked (Figures 24 and 25). The crossing in two directions of such lines provides an excellent check on the accuracy of measurement of features booked on other lines. Line 2 and Line 3 both extend be-yond the nominal end of the line; these extensions may be looked on as offsets extending in the direction of the line and not, as nor-mally, at a right angle to it (Figure 26). They will often be measured for convenience with the linen tape.

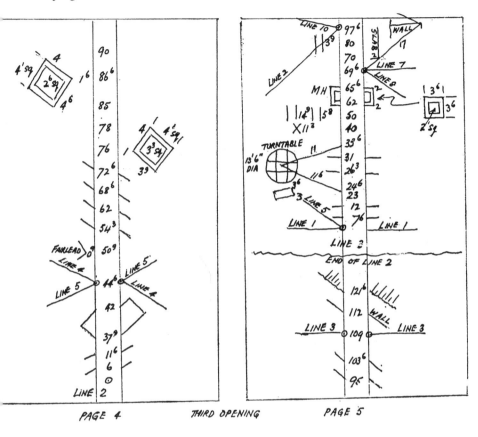

Figs 24 and 25. Pages 4 and 5 of field book notes

Line 4 picks up a number of small features connected with the hydraulic system of the tip and its auxiliary services. Where the detail is complicated, as in the case of the capstan and the hoist jetty, a separate sketch clarifies the detail (Figure 28). Lines 3 and 4 both extend to the edge of the hoist jetty and, here again, the dimensions run to the edge, thus providing a check on the sketch. The remaining lines not only fill in detail and complete the triangulation but, by intersecting the railway track, provide necessary intermediate information on alignment and check the overall accuracy of the survey.

PLOTTING THE SURVEY

The field measurements of our survey have been made to the

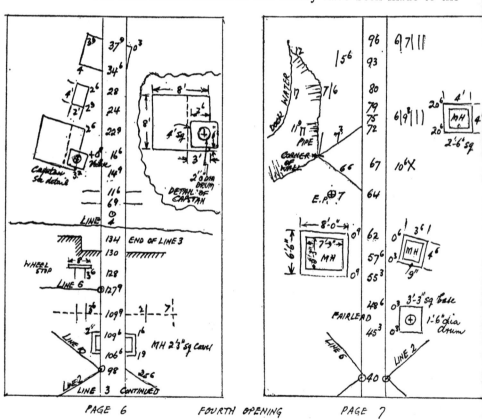

Figs 26 and 27. Pages 6 and 7 of field book notes

nearest 3 in, so that it may be plotted to any scale up to about 10 ft to an inch, or 1/120. Forty feet to an inch (1/480) is a convenient scale for a rather larger area, but the details become small. Twenty feet to an inch (1/240) will allow all the detail measured to be plotted accurately, it will allow a fairly small drawing board to be used and, if the plan is required for reproduction, a reduction of two to one will produce a good photographic block with the lettering remaining clear. The plan reproduced in Figure 28 was plotted to a scale of 1/240 and reduced to half size for the illustration.

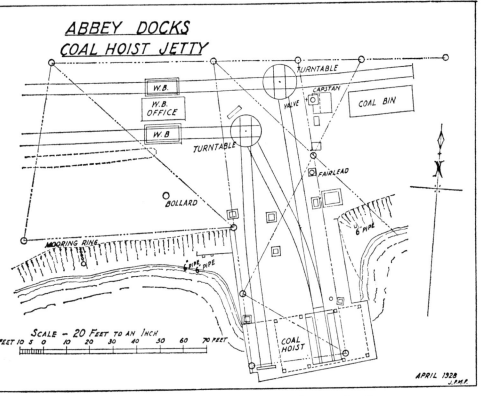

Fig 28. Completed survey of coal-hoist jetty and approach railways

The longest lines of our survey are 169 ft and 134 ft respectively and approximately at right angles to each other. All measured detail on Line 1 is on the survey side so that our work may be expected to plot within an area of paper measuring 169/20, say 8½ in by 134/20, say 7 in. The sheet should be large enough to allow for the title, the drawn scale and the north point, it should also allow for a margin and for trimming, so that a sheet about 15 × 12 in is indicated.

After pinning the paper down, the survey lines may be plotted, using a 2H pencil with a sharp point, starting with Line 1, which is the longest line and conveniently along one edge of the survey. It may therefore be drawn parallel to and about 3 in away from one long edge of the paper. The start of the line, about 4 in from a short edge of the paper, is marked with a dot in a circle, as in the field book. From the field book we take the chainage of 37 ft and mark the start of Line 2, again at 64 ft for Line 4 and at 100 ft for Lines 3 and 5. Finally, at 169 we mark the end of Line 1 and the start of Lines 8 and 9. All these points are shown with the dot in circle symbol. With a pencil compass, having a sharp point, strike out the radii measured in the field book and join the intersections to build up the triangulation of the system of lines. Extend these lines where necessary as indicated in the field book.

At this stage it will be convenient to plot the ties to important fixed points and thus begin our detail plotting. In the case of Line 1, there are the tied corners of the coal bin, the turntable, the corners of weighbridge and office, so that by the time these points are plotted and the details drawn in from the sketches, the first line begins to show some purpose. The permanent-way is plotted by drawing the nearest rail point and by pricking off the 4 ft 8½ in gauge with a small pair of dividers; spring bow dividers are best for this job.

The method of plotting adopted with two scales is to position an appropriate scale alongside the line being plotted, secured by weights, at such distance that the offset scale may be placed with central zero on the line, the two scales then being as shown on Figure 29. If the offset scale is not of the centre zero type, two alternatives are offered; one is to use a division approximately in

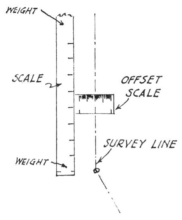

Fig 29. Use of the offset scale

the centre of the scale and work both ways from it; the other is to lay the 'chainage' scale with its edge on the line and plot each side separately. The choice depends to some extent on the length of the offset scale in relation to the longest offset to be measured. Such factors as this are borne in mind by the surveyor when he is doing his field work, always with the ultimate objective of an accurate and easily plotted survey.

As the details are pencilled in, they should be built up to the whole plan progressively as, for instance, the railway track, which may appear to consist of a number of straight lengths instead of a curve, or perhaps a length of straight may have a slight kink, indicating the error in measurement on the ground or in plotting. Such minor errors are usually self-evident and may be corrected. Curves should be faired in by the use of a french curve. All buildings and rectangular objects should be drawn in with the use of two set-

squares, as shown in Figure 30. Buildings may be indicated by
hatching, i.e. with a shading of parallel lines at evenly spaced close
intervals; slopes and banks, if fairly steep—say 1 in 4 or steeper—
may be indicated by 'horse tailing' in the way that the dockside
slopes are indicated on the plotted survey.

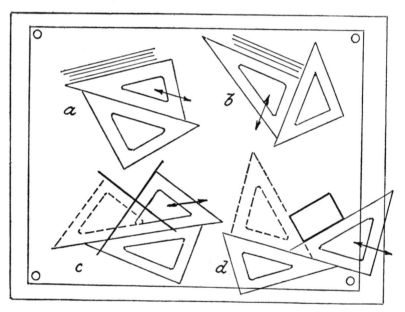

Fig 30. Use of set-squares for drawing parallel lines and lines at
right angles

When the plotting is complete, the survey may be inked in, using
much the same kit of tools as those described in Chapter Five for
inking in mechanical drawing. Lettering should be clear and not
over-elaborate. Larger lettering may be done with pen stencils of
the UNO type, with transfers (Figure 31), or, if the surveyor pre-
fers, it may be done by hand. The small lettering is best done by
hand as this is easier to do neatly in sizes of 1/16 or 3/32 in. A

UNO PEN STENCIL

ABCDEFGHIJL LETRASET
‹ SHEET
abcdefghijlmn   108

Fig 31. Guided lettering: UNO pen stencils and Letraset
transfers

slightly less austere style than that appropriate for mechanical
drawings will be quite acceptable on a survey. Figure 32 shows a
good style which may be achieved with a little practice. In addition
to the title, date and surveyor's signature, no survey is complete
without a drawn scale and a north point.

ABCDEFGHIJKLMNOP
abcdefghijklmnopqrst
1234567890 &

ABCDEFGHIJKLM

ABCDEFGHIJK

Fig. 32. Styles of hand lettering. The first three lines were
done with a steel pen, the fourth with a brush and the fifth
with a felt fountain pen

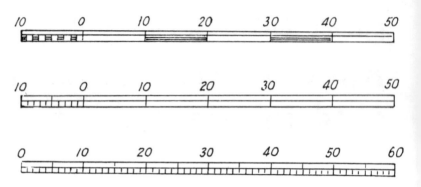

Fig 33. Three types of drawn scales for plans

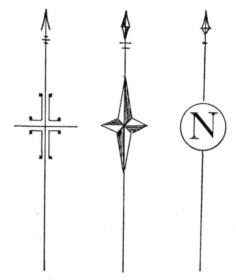

Fig 34. Three simple patterns of north point

The drawn scale may be done in one of the styles given in Figure 33 and may be pricked in from the chainage scale used in plotting the survey. It not only provides a means of scaling off dimensions or distances with dividers, but also provides the means of checking distortion of the plan under changing conditions of weather. The north point may be taken from the field book data or, if that is not available, it may be taken by comparison with an appropriate Ordnance Sheet. This may be done by transferring the angle between due north and a line between two prominent objects common to the survey and the Ordnance plan of the same area. The north point should not be over-elaborate, but otherwise may be of a pattern to the fancy of the surveyor. It may be located anywhere on the plan, so that it may fill in a void and so balance the layout of the sheet (Figure 34).

CHAPTER FIVE

Measuring up Machines and Structures

T HE industrial archaeologist untrained in mechanical drawing will sooner or later wish to measure and draw a machine of apparent complication, but may feel that the task is beyond his powers. He should not be daunted, as the most involved mechanism consists of a system of comparatively simple units, each based on ordinary geometrical forms, such as the cube, cylinder, or cone, all easy to draw in proper relationship. This is always done by using a method of conventional presentation, known as 'orthographic projection'.

The land surveyor deals with the surface of the earth which, to his scale of working, may be considered flat, or at most in low relief. This he may draw on a flat sheet as a plan, indicating variations in height by simple symbols. A machine or building is an object in three dimensions, all having an equal degree of importance, and it must be drawn on a two-dimensional sheet. This is done by a series of *views*, each of which is related to an imaginary plane surface, so that, just as the land surveyor bases his survey on a pattern of *lines*, the mechanical engineer or architect needs to set up a pattern of *surfaces*.

These plane surfaces are usually at right angles to each other; in fact, the word 'orthographic' has Greek origins meaning 'right-angled drawing'. Although it was known in a general sense by artists such as Albrecht Durer in the sixteenth century, or even earlier, it has only been formalized as 'engineering drawing' for little more than a century.

The ultimate aim of measuring up a machine or building is usually to produce a drawing; the drawing will be displayed by orthographic projection, and our approach to the task is therefore dictated by the end requirement. Figure 35 shows a small object, a

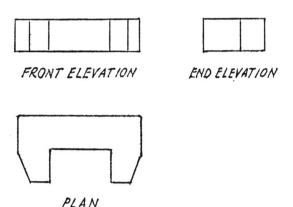

FRONT ELEVATION   END ELEVATION

PLAN

Fig 35. Elevations and plan of the gib piece

gib piece, in relation to three plane surfaces, each of which is at right angles to the other two. A *view* may be projected on to each plane which will be a representation of those details of the object visible to the eye in a position normal to the plane. The example shown has the *object between* the eye and the plane: this is known as

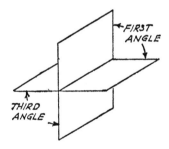

Fig 36. Angles of first- and third-angle projection

first-angle projection. It is also permissible to draw with the *plane surface*, in imagination, between the object and the eye and this is known as *third-angle* projection. These two formalities are indicated in Figure 36. In our example, if we hinge our two vertical planes and swing them down to a common plane surface, we get the result shown in Figure 37, with the three views shown as a *plan* and two *elevations*, the orthographic projection of our object.

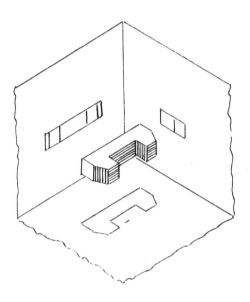

Fig 37. Projection of gib piece

This is a simple case, but is sufficient to show that our measurements must be related to a series of plane surfaces, the principal ones being mutually at right angles. The whole subject is worked out very fully and a number of excellent textbooks on engineering drawing are available, some being referred to in the Bibliography for this chapter. In almost every case, the drawing of a machine or structure is made before it is built and the usual textbook is written with that in view. The reverse process, of measuring an existing object for recording on a drawing, is largely one of creating our imaginary plane surfaces and measuring our object in relation to them. The equipment required for measuring up a three-dimensional object such as an engine or a building may vary within wide limits. These depend on such factors as the size of the object, its degree of complication and the accuracy required in the finished drawing. As we are not measuring with the intention of ordering interchangeable spare parts or for the purpose of building an exact working replica, it may be assumed that fairly simple equipment will suffice. As in the case of land surveying, the value of the finished drawing will depend more on the use of sound methods than on expensive kits of tools.

A more serious problem which may arise is that of accessibility, for instance of internal details of engines such as cylinder bores, of mill gearing and wheels hidden under floors, or the hidden structural features of buildings. It may become necessary to make an approximate estimate of the size of certain details after a study of the contemporary literature. Much of the early design of machines was based on trial and error, the results of successful efforts being recorded in such books as Bourne's *Treatise on the Steam Engine*, which gives tables of dimensions recommended for engines in a great range of sizes and varieties. Sometimes, of course, it will be possible to dismantle the machine, especially if it is destined for scrap. In this case, the owner or the scrap merchant may agree to allow a quick measuring up and photography before or during the breaking-up period.

TOOLS REQUIRED

The tools and equipment described here may be considered enough for most eventualities and may not all be required on every occasion. The craftsman buying tools to last a lifetime is anxious to obtain the best quality, but the spare-time industrial archaeologist will probably find less costly tools suffice.

Measures of length will call for a tape measure similar to that recommended for land surveying in Chapter Four. In addition, a steel strip tape, of the self-supporting variety, 6 ft long when fully extended, will provide for general rough measurements. This tape should be the kind which has a 2-in square case, this being most useful when taking internal measurements. A 12-in steel rule, preferably stainless, with fractional parts of an inch down to sixteenths on one edge and decimal divisions to hundredths on the other, will complete our length-measuring tools.

Calipers, both inside and outside, are essential for measuring diameters; the spring variety are so much easier to use that the extra cost is worthwhile. One pair each of the 4-in size will meet most requirements (Figure 38), but a pair of 6- or 8-in outside

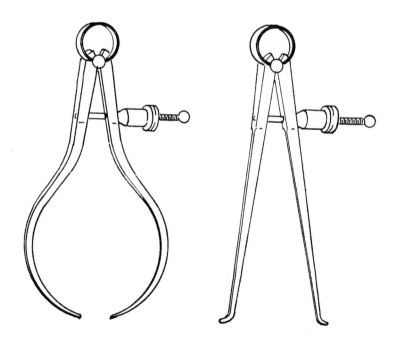

Fig 38. Outside and inside spring calipers

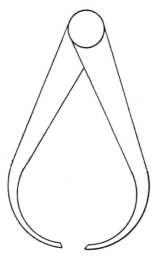

Fig 39. Firm joint calipers

calipers of the friction-joint variety may often be found useful (Figure 39).

At least one square is necessary, of the kind shown in Figure 40. Quite inexpensive ones are obtainable today and they serve a great variety of purposes. The blade is graduated and slides in the stock;

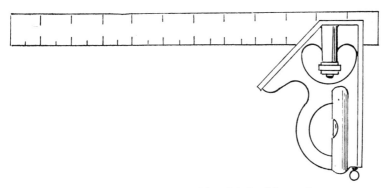

Fig 40. Sliding square with spirit-level in stock

G

it may be used as a depth or height gauge. The stock carries a spirit level so that it may also be used as a plumb rule.

Angles may be measured with a bevel gauge in conjunction with a protractor; the latter may be semicircular and of an inexpensive variety, while the bevel gauge may be of the type found in any carpenter's tool kit, although a universal bevel gauge can be advantageous at times.

A straight-edge will frequently be found useful, and at times essential. Although a steel one is best, for most purposes of recording dimensions within the scope of industrial archaeology, hardwood will often be adequate and has the advantage that a suitable length and section may be made up to suit the circumstances. In conjunction with the straight-edge, a spirit level and a plumb bob will often be required.

A surface or height gauge, used in conjunction with a surface plate, will be found useful when separate components are being measured. It may also be used for measuring distances from a clear flat surface, such as the height of centres from a flat lathe bed. For a surface plate, a piece of plate glass serves admirably.

In addition to the gear listed above, various articles will be needed to meet each case, such as a string line, hammer and nails and a few 'G' cramps, mostly for establishing datum lines from which to measure.

Notes should be taken in square-paper notebooks, while more careful sketches should be made on a square-paper sketch pad. These are obtainable in a great variety of sizes and rulings. The best ruling for most purposes is inches and tenths. Fractional dimensions may be converted to decimals and, before very long, the recorder will find himself able to convert any fraction down to thirty-seconds from memory. The use of squared paper for such sketches was developed to a fine art by Isambard Kingdom Brunel, whose sketch books are preserved in the library of Bristol University. Bound in hard covers, the books opened out to a squared sheet of about 12 by 18 in within margins. Inside the cover of each book is stuck a piece of coarse sandpaper and one of fine emery cloth, for Brunel to sharpen his pencils on—a useful tip for the user of pencils, although the finer variety of ball pen has many advantages. In the black variety, sketches may be reproduced by any of the modern document-copying processes. For quick sketching of machine parts, or even complete machines of simple construction, isometric scaled paper may be found useful. This is ruled with a pattern of equilateral triangles instead of squares and, with it, one view will often be sufficient for recording the details required to scale.

A device which is rather more elaborate than the sketch book and which may be used for the production of scale drawings quickly is called the Quickdraw, illustrated in Figure 41. It will be seen to consist of a pantograph drawing instrument carrying a specially designed template of transparent plastic which enables the most frequently used angles to be drawn. It is divided with inch and metric scales and also has a range of bevelled-edge holes from 3/32 to 1 in diameter for the quick drawing of small circles. It is produced in a portfolio form of 14 in square, or as a separate tool with pantograph arms of 15 in length to be attached to a drawing board.

SKETCHING MACHINE DETAILS

As a general rule when sketching a piece of machinery, the general arrangement or layout would be drawn first, details of the machine requiring more adequate treatment being dealt with afterwards. For a clearer explanation, it will be better to reverse this procedure and describe the sketching of simple details before embarking on an account of the measurement of a complete machine.

MAKING THE FAIR DRAWING

The student of industrial history will, if he is able, take every

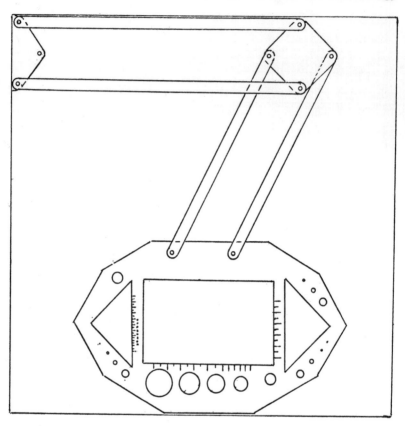

Fig 41. Quickdraw drafting apparatus

opportunity of looking at contemporary drawings of early industrial machinery. Only the original drawings, many of them works of art of no mean quality, will convey a full understanding of the meticulous skill and care put into this work by draughtsmen a century or more ago. The war of 1914–18 probably marked the end of the fine draughtsmanship of the Industrial Revolution, for during those years it became necessary rapidly to step up the production of many objects of hardware, and although the accuracy of the end product may have improved, the time absorbed in producing highly finished detailed drawings could not contribute to the war effort. However, the First and Second World Wars merely accelerated the changes which would anyway have taken place and which were due to a number of factors. Among these were the greater complication of the machines to be drawn; higher wages of draughtsmen, which added greatly to the cost of drawings; photo-copying methods which enabled drawing offices to produce good readable prints from pencil tracings; stencilling aids to lettering. The modern drawing office has an output far exceeding anything envisaged by engineers a century ago. These drawings enable the workshops to make numbers of identical or at any rate interchangeable parts; the manufacturer can market a vast array of goods which make our present civilization what it is.

While it is not suggested that he can achieve the superb standard of workmanship displayed in some of the old engineering drawings stored up in the plan rooms of many long-established undertakings, the industrial archaeologist may with advantage attempt to achieve a workmanlike finish to his drawings and, by doing so, appreciate more fully the virtuosity displayed by a first-class draughtsman.

DRAWING INSTRUMENTS

The enormous demand for instruments for geometrical drawing created by schools, technical colleges and universities, as well as drawing offices generally, has enabled the instrument-making industry to provide, by mass production, drawing instruments of high quality at astonishingly low prices. There is no need to use poor instruments for high quality work when the good stuff is available in such abundance, especially as the number of pieces of equipment required by the industrial archaeologist is quite small.

The one item on which a compromise may be made in this

respect is the drawing board. Those for professional work are usually constructed of softwood secured to battens at the back to prevent warping and provided with a hardwood edge of ebony or similar timber to take the wear of the tee-square. Plywood drawing boards, until recent years, were not considered satisfactory, but with the advantage of synthetic glues a board of the best quality plywood, a $\frac{1}{2}$ in or more thick and carefully squared along the edges, will prove satisfactory. A board to take 'imperial' sheets of drawing paper (30 by 22 in) will be adequate and for many purposes 'half imperial' (22 by 15 in) will serve.

A tee-square of the best quality will last a lifetime and should be of mahogany with ebony edge, 23 in. size for half imperial or 31 in for imperial-size drawing board (Figure 42). Set-squares should be of transparent plastic, 8 in size, one of 45 degrees and one of 30–60

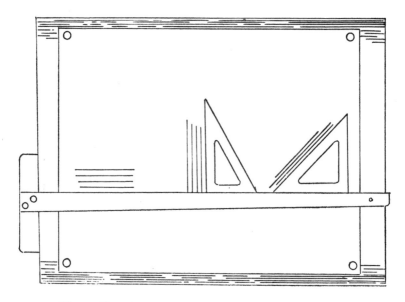

Fig 42. Use of drawing board, tee-square and set-squares

degrees. A larger, say 12 in size, 30–60 degrees set-square can be found very useful as the long (hypotenuse) edge serves as a straight-edge.

For measuring angles, a protractor is needed. This should, for preference, be the circular or semicircular kind in transparent plastic; 6 in diameter will be adequate. A convenient although possibly more expensive alternative is an adjustable set-square which has a scale of 0 to 45 degrees.

A french curve of suitable shape will be one of the most useful items, especially when tracing. It should be of transparent plastic and 6 to 9 in long.

Fig 43. French curve—there are many other patterns

Scales may, in general, follow the description in Chapter Four; but, whereas those for plotting surveys will usually be to representative fractions (RF) corresponding to Ordnance scales, or up to perhaps 8 ft to an inch $(\frac{1}{96})$ at the largest, mechanical drawings usually range from the $(\frac{1}{96})$ scale to full size $(\frac{1}{1})$, or in the case of tiny components even larger than full size. For the drawing board, the same principles apply as in plotting a survey; always remembering that a clear scale, to one fraction only, fully divided along its length and numbered left and right on opposite sides, is the type least likely to lead to errors.

Although instruments may be purchased separately and without the usual enclosing case, it is probably best for the beginner to purchase what is known as a half set of compasses, complete with case;

the latter may be stiff or flexible. The half set includes compasses with interchangeable pen, pencil and divider points, together with an extension piece for increasing the maximum working radius; 4 in size would be appropriate (Figure 44). If a suitable half set is offered with a matching pair of dividers and a drawing pen, these may with

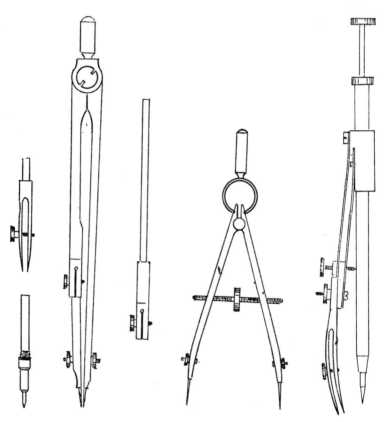

Left to right:
Fig 44. Half set of compasses
Fig 45. Spring bow dividers
Fig 46. Sliding or pump centre pen bows

advantage be obtained as part of the set. Small bows, as shown in Figure 45, should be confined to dividers only, for pricking off short distances such as the width of a gauge of permanent-way for a railway survey, or for rivet spacing on a drawing of a boiler. For drawing very small circles, especially in ink, the sliding or pump centre compass shown in Figure 46 is much easier to use, as the centre may be placed in position and firmly held down with the first finger while the compass pen or pencil is lowered to touch the paper and then twirled round with thumb and second finger. There is no tendency for the centre to jump from the paper and the smallest circles may be drawn without trouble.

MEASURING AND RECORDING

With the immense variety of machinery which enters within the scope of industrial archaeology, it is difficult to lay down any rules for procedure in measuring and recording. There are, however, some helpful basic principles. In many instances, where problems of congestion and complication of parts have to be overcome, a great deal of improvisation and resourcefulness will be required, but so long as the measurer can obtain actual physical access, he can usually determine the principal physical dimensions of a machine, its layout and some details of its component parts.

The first essential to keep in mind is the formal pattern of plane surfaces to which the finished drawing will be referred. In most instances these will, in practice, be true horizontal and vertical planes, although in exceptional cases it may be expedient to use other plane surfaces as references. Many, if not most, mechanical assemblies include suitable reference planes built in, from which all measurements may be taken. This may be the surface of a lathe bed or the work-table of a drilling machine. A steam engine will have many planed faces, such as the crosshead guides or the planed faces to which the column bases are bolted. The cylinder faces may be lagged, but if not, the top face of the cylinder covers may provide a machined face to which a straight-edge may be clamped, from which, in turn, a plumb line may be suspended. The flat faces of a flywheel are also useful references.

A number of reference faces may be used within a complicated layout and, if this is done, care must be taken to measure the relationship between the faces. It should not be assumed that the floor, walls, or ceiling of a factory or mill are true either in the horizontal or vertical planes. If these are proved to be so by checking with level, straight-edge, square and plumb bob, then they will prove valuable reference surfaces. Systems of line shafting are usually reliable as the successful operation of belt drives is dependent on correct alignment, and the millwright may be relied on for seeing to this. Line shafts also carry pulleys, the faces of which provide reference planes at a right angle to the axis of the line shaft.

All dimensions, however obtained, should be checked against an overall dimension. Wherever possible it is better to pick up running dimensions measured from one end or face of an assembly, but as this is not always practicable, intermediate measurements should be added up and compared with a length, height or width measured independently. The use of squared paper will assist greatly in preventing serious errors being made in site measurements, as the sketch made to scale will tend to prove the correctness or otherwise of the measurements. Errors may creep in by the measurer forgetting to add or deduct half the diameter when using a shaft as a reference or when measuring the throw of a crank.

Figure 47 shows the main dimensions required in measuring a horizontal steam engine for the purposes of drawing an elevation. Once these dimensions are established, other details may be measured from them without fear of serious error creeping in. In this case, the position of the vertical height of the centre line of the motion is established in relation to the horizontal foundation and the horizontal measurements (a), (b) and (c + d) carefully estab-

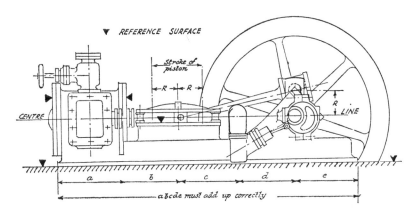

Fig 47. Side elevation of horizontal steam engine, showing reference surfaces from which other dimensions may be taken

lished. The length of stroke is twice the throw, or radius, of the crankshaft centre and may be checked by the signs of wear made by the crosshead in the guides, deducting the length of the crosshead from the marks on the guides or on the oil film. If the engine is in use, many of the dimensions will be known by the maintenance staff; the bore of the cylinder, for instance, will not call for opening up. If, in the case of an old engine, the cylinder cover cannot be removed, the bore may be estimated quite accurately by assuming that the pitch circle diameter of the cover bolts is located exactly midway in the width of the flange or bolting face (Figure 48).

If a machine is known to have been working up to a recent date, then the squareness and truth of its parts may be fairly taken for granted. If, however, it has been lying idle for a considerable time, the truth of reference faces such as flywheels should be checked in their relationship to other parts of the machine (Figure 49). Each case must be dealt with on its merits; the walls and floor of an engine-house may be true and plumb, as are those of the 1840 Terminus Station at Southampton of the London & Southampton Railway. Designed by Tite, the execution was so perfect that a local

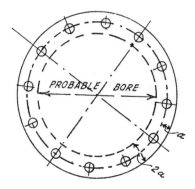

Fig 48. Cylinder cover of steam engine, showing how the
probable bore may be estimated

nautical-instrument maker used the building as a reference when
checking sextants.

It may not always be possible to measure up all the details of a
machine or structure in one visit. This will not matter if the main
reference planes are established and, if necessary, marked in some
way, much as a land surveyor establishes reference points in relation
to established buildings of a permanent nature, or drives pegs into
the ground where no suitable references exist. Ruined and un-

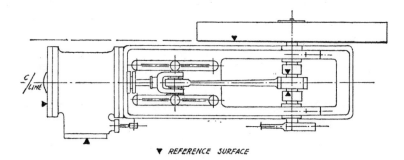

Fig 49. Plan of horizontal steam engine, showing reference
surfaces from which measurements may be taken

occupied buildings offer no difficulty as marks may freely be made, but in the case of buildings in use, the manner of making reference points recognizable must be approved by the occupier who is not usually likely to object to an occasional pencil mark or panel pin driven into the woodwork. He must be asked first and the traces removed on the close of the survey.

A PRACTICAL EXAMPLE

At the head of Southampton Water, in the ancient parish of Eling, are a tide mill and causeway, the property of Winchester College for more than five centuries (Plate 7). The mill-wheels have not revolved by water power since 1936, but between the wars a diesel engine provided energy for the millstones and auxiliary machinery. The mill ceased to work in 1946. Some of the power transmission gearing is still there, however, as well as two pairs of millstones and some auxiliary equipment (Plate 8). It is probable that this will be removed in the near future, so that an endeavour is being made to record its layout and details.

As in most mills, the grain flows downward and it must therefore be lifted in sacks to the loft to start its journey back, through the mill, to ground level. The main power supply provides, through auxiliary shafting, the energy to operate sack hoists, and the accompanying sketches and finished drawing show the arrangement and details of this drive and the method of taking power from the main vertical shaft.

The mill had two main water-wheels, each operating in a tunnel under the floor of the building, and each driving through bevel gearing a vertical shaft which continued to the ceiling joists of the first floor. At this point, a bearing was provided to take the top end of the vertical shafts, each of which carried a large crown wheel with mortise teeth driving cast iron pinions keyed to the ends of auxiliary shafts. Plate 9 shows this gear and pinion arrangement.

The sketch, Figure 50, shows the details as recorded at the mill, in conditions of semi-darkness, with little on which to base an alignment except the vertical and horizontal shafting, the latter having been aligned with packing between the hanger flanges and the joists to compensate for sag which had developed in the age-long loading of the upper floor. The crown wheel and pinion details were ascertained with calipers, steel-strip tape and stainless-steel rule. The joist spacing and hanger centres were established and the height of the shafting from the floor, although this figure was only approximate to the nearest inch owing to the condition of the floor. The strip tape was adequate for these measurements, but a linen tape was used to check the overall correctness of the intermediate dimensions.

For details such as the hangers, pinions and gear teeth, the strip tape, steel rule and spring calipers were used, the latter being of the type shown in Figure 38. For the main shaft, however, it was necessary to use a larger pair, and these were of the firm-joint variety shown in Figure 39.

The number of teeth on the main crown wheel were counted between the centres of the six arms of the main casting, there being fifteen teeth, centre to centre: thus $15 \times 6 = 90$, a much surer method than trying to count right round the wheel. In the present instance, all the teeth were accessible and could have been counted, marking every tenth tooth with chalk, but in many cases it is not possible to reach the whole circumference of a large gear wheel. All the teeth in the pinions were counted, the odd figure of twenty-one being to provide a *hunting tooth*; these ensure that any wear due to irregularities in the pinions is evened out and the hornbeam-wood teeth of the crown wheel all wear down at the same rate.

It will be noted that details of components such as the hangers are separately sketched if necessary, to a larger scale and filling in odd spaces on the sheet. Such sketches may occupy separate pages of a notebook if this is used for sketching.

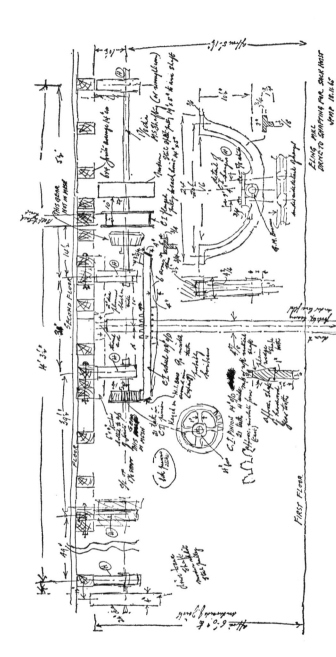

Fig 50. Sketch layout and details of the auxiliary machinery at Eling Mill. Done on squared paper (inches and tenths) in the badly lighted mill

The example given (Figure 51) is a simple one and it did not call for great ingenuity or accuracy in measurement. More elaborate installations consist, as a rule, merely of a series of such simple assemblies: if each sub-assembly is tackled separately, the whole machine or complicated layout may be sketched without difficulty. Time, care and common sense will enable the investigator to sketch assemblies such as this one and thus provide a record of one more vanishing detail of our industrial past.

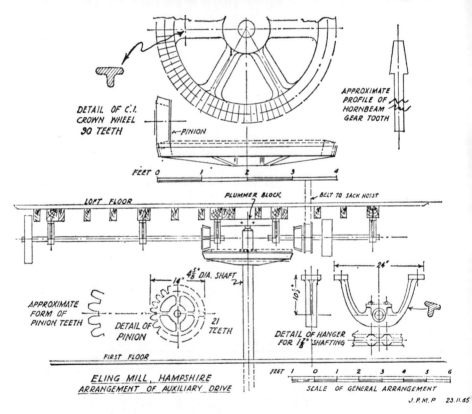

Fig 51. Finished sketch to scale of the auxiliary machinery at Eling Mill

NOTES ON MEASURING BUILDINGS AND STRUCTURES

When the novice is debating the conflicting aspects of measuring and recording an apparently complicated building of importance to the industrial or social historian, his diffidence may be overcome by adopting the outlook already recommended to the measurer of machines. There are few buildings, however large and apparently involved in detail, which cannot be reduced to a series of sub-divisions for the purposes of measuring and recording. Indeed, in the case of many structures of appreciable age, these subdivisions, if looked for, will at the same time disclose stages in development, and possibly change of use. Mere size in itself need not daunt any-one, as many great mills and similar buildings have a dignified simplicity and solidity which free them from some of the traps for the measurer which are to be found in smaller, less substantial buildings.

Some of the most frequent of such traps are associated with lack of plumbness in walls and squareness in plans; floor levels are also suspect, especially in mining areas where subsidence is ever-lurking, although the author has found instances in modern building where the floor of a room is as much as 3 in higher at one corner than at the corner opposite. Any wall may be suspect if it includes evidence of bracing or of tie rods; it is then probable that the roof trusses have tended to spread the walls or that sagging floors due to overloading have caused a tendency for the walls to buckle inwards.

The siting of a building often dictates the shape of its plan; rooms are not necessarily square, and the test for this is to check *both* diagonals when measuring the internal dimensions. Not only may a building or part of it, be out of square, but its outer walls may con-ceal unexpected irregularities due to origins long forgotten. The author's father, when a young pupil of Mr James Inglis (later Sir James), suffered much heart-searching when he measured a build-ing in the old part of Plymouth. After allowing for reasonable wall

H

thicknesses, the inside and outside dimensions showed a discrepancy of 14 ft: further investigation showed that the building and its neighbours were built into the ancient town wall, which must have been about 15 ft thick. This may seem to be an extreme case, but there are many such; the ancient Saxon church of St Laurence in Bradford-on-Avon was lost for many centuries through the development of buildings around—and into—it. An industrial building may include a bricked-up chimney base or an unrecorded furnace totally enclosed and lost in the passage of time.

Bricked-up windows and doors should be looked for. Many trades based on home labour needed all the natural light possible, and therefore the work was carried out in upper-floor rooms with continuous windows. In subsequent years, the cost of maintenance and other factors led to the reduction of glazed areas and their substitution by brickwork. The later brickwork may usually be recognized, and from this the original use of the building discovered.

Sometimes an inquiry into structural change may bring an unexpected explanation. Many years ago a well-known firm of West Country engineers decided to rearrange their workshops, including the blacksmiths' shop. During the clean-up of that workshop, an iron plate was removed, which had been leaning against the wall for

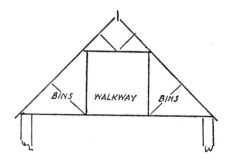

Fig 52. Roof arrangement of Eling Mill

some years, and this disclosed a hole in the brick wall leading to the conveniently situated pub next door.

The roof spaces should be explored if possible; these offered useful under-cover accommodation. The roof trusses at Eling Mill are of the queen post type, in order to allow the maximum headroom for a walkway down the centre line of the roof, while the remaining side spaces were occupied with corn bins and hoppers (Figure 52). The unusual in roof construction is always worth recording; quite recently, a conference on timber engineering at Southampton received an interesting paper by a Scandinavian professor on his

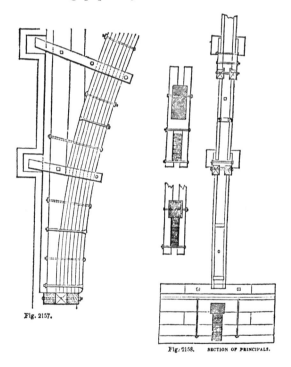

Fig. 2157.

Fig. 2158.   SECTION OF PRINCIPALS.

Fig 53. Laminated timber arch of about 1830 from Cresy's
Cyclopaedia of Civil Engineering

original work in the design of laminated timber arch roofs. On a
visit to inspect interesting buildings, he was shown, to his surprise,
a laminated timber arch roof construction in a building erected in
1866. Figure 53 shows an illustration of this form of construction
taken from Cresy's *Cyclopaedia*, published in 1847. The use of iron,
cast or wrought, in building construction may disclose novel applications in design, while even the modern materials, steel and reinforced concrete, had their early conservative days, during which
strange designs were put into construction.

CHAPTER SIX

Keeping a Record

NATURE is a scavenger; otherwise, the face of the earth would have long ago been overwhelmed by the remains of its teeming life. The processes that put dead trees, animals and ultimately rocks, back into the soil are equally effective in returning our roads, bridges and factories to a natural state; but as these processes are slow, it is more usual for man to destroy his own works and build them anew in his progressive development. For many centuries little or no regard was held for any historical value in the objects being demolished. Today our growing prosperity, and the higher standard of education that this makes possible, has made us very aware of the debt we owe to the past: and from this has come a reluctance to part with the objects created by our forefathers. At the same time, the exponential rate of material progress is calling for more frequent replacement of those same artifacts, so that we are faced with the problem of how much we should preserve, not only of the objects themselves, but also of the growing mass of paper and other records associated with them in their relation to society.

As we are only able to preserve a proportion of this heritage, it is incumbent on us to keep as much evidence as we can in such forms and proportions that historians of the future will be able to build up true pictures of the past generations. This will require, even by minimum standards, a vast amount of material, some of which will necessarily be of large size, such as buildings, transport relics—canals, railways and roads—or even such things as sewage-disposal works. The highest degree of selectivity will be needed in deciding which of such large occupiers of space shall be preserved; obviously, as a rule only those which are most representative of their period can be kept. The intermediate class of objects, the kind that can be stored under museum conditions, must also be carefully chosen. Taking motor transport as an example, even one car of each model produced will eventually present the museum authorities with a major storage problem; similar instances may be taken from almost every human activity.

The written records themselves, by their very bulk, are already creating difficulties in storage and indexing; in the present-day spate of paper only the specialist can know of all that is available, even in his own ever-narrowing field. The task of the industrial archaeologist is to work closely with students of all aspects of our past history and to guide them on what should be preserved, what needs reducing to forms such as summaries, tables, or graphs, and what may be destroyed. The ultimate aim is to reduce the mass, while preserving the facts, but for some time to come it will probably be best to preserve too much rather than too little. As time goes on, the techniques of recording are likely to improve greatly and overlapping collections may be redistributed, written and pictorial records put on tape, and the whole system of preservation and recording linked with industry, education and, possibly, the use of leisure time.

To the industrial archaeologist, the printed recording of his activities must be the ultimate aim. Whether his findings be the result of field work or the co-ordination of library and museum studies with personal expert knowledge of a trade or profession, diffidence should not prevent the student from publishing them in some form. Furthermore, publication should not be delayed too long. A worker in the study of some branch of industry or commerce may spend a lifetime on his chosen subject, amassing facts, opinions and illustrations. A good book may be written on the basis of ten to twenty years' work; but in that time, the information being gained may be of great use to another worker in the same field. The best solution is to publish as you go, by papers to appropriate societies, articles in the local or specialist press, or even an occasional letter to the correspondence columns of the same periodicals.

The author has often been asked the question: how long does it take to write a book? The literal answer would probably be six to twelve months, but the material has more likely been accumulating in the author's files, cupboards and experience, for twenty years or more. A good example of this is shown by a recently published study of a canal system, *London's Lost Route to the Sea* by P. A. L. Vine (David & Charles). In the preface to this work, published in 1965, the author describes his first interest in his study, which began in 1942 and which has involved him in field and archive work continuously since that time. In his own words, quoted from the preface:

> Facts and figures have to be painstakingly gleaned from the dusty ledgers and account books of the individual companies, from parliamentary papers, petitions, minute books, shareholders' registers, newspaper files and miscellaneous correspondence, while a field study of the works of the navigations and conversations with the inhabitants who live about their banks may help to provide missing evidence and local colour.

Each of the chapters in this book contains material for a paper to one or other of the societies interested in social or industrial history.

PUBLISHED PAPERS

The publication of a paper presented to a local society is usually the means whereby an investigator makes known the results of work in the field of industrial archaeology. Many such societies hold meetings in the winter, when field work is curtailed by bad weather and short days. Papers of interest presented at such meetings are then printed or otherwise produced as a bulletin or a newsletter, or in a more ambitious society as proceedings. Very short communications which include new facts, or a revised opinion on already known material, are welcomed by such societies; their publication ensures that some published record is made, and in practically all cases this is stored in a suitable repository such as the local library for the benefit of future students. A student of industrial archaeology need feel no diffidence in presenting the results of his work in this form; the editor of a society's bulletin will guide him on matters of style and presentation. If his paper is read at a meeting, the courteous introduction by a chairman and the wording of a vote of thanks, will encourage the most reticent author to pursue his work to a further stage and then present the results.

In due course, the industrial archaeologist will be encouraged to offer a paper to an organization of national standing. It may be the Newcomen Society, whose papers are consistently of a high order of quality and cover a wide range of subjects in the field of industrial history and archaeology. Apart from societies which specialize in history, many professional, commercial and trade organizations welcome an occasional contribution to their winter programme on the history and background of their own sub-section of our civilization. These societies will always give guidance to authors and lecturers on the preparation and presentation of their papers.

Such methods of recording intermediate results of a long study have more than one advantage. Not only does the author of a paper inform fellow-workers in his own field of his existence and activities, thus often saving duplication of effort, but he may also attract to his own notice the special knowledge or experience of experts in a branch of industry who may offer advice of great help in his investigations. It is usually of advantage to work backwards in historical studies, and the acquaintance of experts in modern industry may often be turned to advantage when an opinion is required on a problem arising in the study of early technology. Such opinions are often freely expressed in the discussion of a paper on the history of an industry.

To achieve its object a report, press article, or paper to be read at a meeting must be written in a style appropriate to its subject, with its component parts marshalled in due order. A report of results arising from a study in industrial archaeology will probably follow similar lines to a report on an investigation into an equivalent problem in modern technology. It would start with a statement describing the object of the study, and this would be followed by an outline of the knowledge of the subject available before the project is started. An account in some detail of the investigation itself will probably form the core of most documents of this kind, describing the equipment and personnel employed, techniques adopted, difficulties encountered and special permissions required for access to premises or to archive stores. The actual data resulting from the study should then be discussed and any conclusions drawn be given, with references to those parts of the study leading to the conclusions.

A fairly long paper may commence with a paragraph which summarizes the object and results of the study. This will enable a searcher to discover whether the paper is likely to provide material in his own particular field, and will also help the librarian or abstractor who is compiling reference works for students in future days. It might be on the following lines:

> This paper describes an investigation carried out during weekends in the summer of 1965 at the site of the derelict foundry in Exe Street, Upford, to ascertain, if possible, the range of goods manufactured and the techniques employed. The main casting-shop foundations were uncovered, together with the remains of two furnaces. A scrap dump was discovered and the relics from this show that the main product of the foundry was castings for builders' supplies and farm equipment. Traces of an earlier building were discovered and it is intended to continue the investigation into these during the summer of 1966.

HOUSE MAGAZINES

The modern attitude in management, leading toward better staff relationships, has made the staff magazine an important link in the communications system. No such journal would survive, however, on a mixture of management exhortation, personal notes and cross-word puzzles; editors are constantly searching for interesting and readable material with which to fill their columns. Many firms circulate the staff magazine to customers, when it soon becomes a friendly link with them also. Not only is the history of the sponsoring firm of interest to staff and customer alike, but also the history of the whole industry, indeed, one might say of the whole of industry. The industrial archaeologist starting with a letter to the correspondence column of his firm's magazine may soon find himself a regular contributor to its other columns, and from thence, to the pages of more widely circulated journals.

ILLUSTRATIONS

Although many aspects of industrial history may be discussed adequately without pictorial illustrations, industrial archaeology almost invariably demands maps and pictures. As sources of information these have been discussed in Chapter Three, and many of the comments there apply to maps used to illustrate points or arguments in a published paper or book. Very often, however, it will be desirable to prepare maps specially, as by this means topographical details may be stressed in accordance with their importance and irrelevant details may be omitted altogether.

The requirements of printing techniques must be kept in mind when tracing or drawing maps for reproduction. It is rarely practicable to draw maps to the size of the space available on the column or page; usually the original is from two to four times the size. If the original map or sketch is drawn to an even multiple of the dimensions available for the reduction much time will be saved in setting up the work. The page or column size of the finished paper thus bears a direct relationship to the sketch size, and the editor will assist his authors in deciding on the original dimensions to be adopted for maps. If a number of illustrations are being supplied,

L

it is a great help to the blockmaker to be able to photograph several at the same time to the same degree of reduction.

The degree of reduction must be considered when lettering is done. Most amateur cartographers will probably use some form of aid to their lettering: this is to be recommended, as nothing spoils a map or plan more than poor lettering. Pen stencils of the UNO type are easy to use and are very clear; transfer lettering is now available in most art shops in a wide range of styles. Whichever is chosen, the degree of reduction must be allowed for. This is especially important in the case of letters having closed loops, such as a, b, d, e and o; all these tend to attract ink into the loops when printed, to the detriment of clarity. The same allowance must be made when drawing the lines of the original map: not only is the line thickness reduced, but if the original line is too thin, parts of it may disappear altogether on the reduced plan. Not only must the line thickness be considered, but the space between lines must be sufficient to prevent the effect of capillarity carrying ink from one line to another. This also applies to cross-hatching which, if possible, is best avoided altogether; if it is unavoidable, it should be done with lines almost at right angles to each other. Cross-hatching with lines at an acute angle will inevitably result in unsightly blobs or, if the printer uses a very fluffy paper, in a solid black mass. When drawing the map or plan, do not omit the north point and the drawn scale. It will probably be better to omit all reference to the actual scale, describing the drawn scale only in terms of SCALE OF FEET or SCALE OF MILES, not as 1/500 or as FOUR FEET TO AN INCH. Layout is important; the overall proportions in relation to the finished page size should not be encroached on by the title, scale, or north point. If the plan is well designed, all these can usually be fitted in to give a well-balanced appearance. If necessary, consider carefully whether some unimportant part may be sacrificed so that the whole plan may not have to be so severely scaled down when reproduced.

Not only maps, but other drawn illustrations may be produced as line blocks; so may reductions of handbills or woodcuts and manuscripts such as letters, minute-book or account-book pages. Half-tones must be printed on a smooth art paper and therefore— unless the whole book is printed on such paper—are grouped at intervals throughout the book, or possibly at the end of the book. Line drawings may be printed close to the matter being discussed, thus enabling the reader to refer to description and illustration on the same page. For this reason, clear line drawings are often to be preferred to photographs.

SKETCHING AND DRAWING

Many people who pursue some form of fieldwork in industrial archaeology are afraid of attempting any form of sketching or drawing. The absence of formal training need be no barrier to the production of an adequate sketch note in a notebook or on the rear side of record cards.

The simplest type of sketch is the strictly elevational one of a building or piece of machinery. This is usually drawn with a soft pencil in the industrial archaeologist's notebook; in black ink or black 'ball-point' on a record card. The proportions of the various elements of a building or machine can be determined by gauging the relative size of these using the pencil as a scale when held at arm's length. Figure 54 shows a drawing of this kind with an enlargement of the detail. This is a horse wheel in its associated building which stood at Shabden Park near Croydon. Figure 55 is a drawing prepared by Lawrence Cameron of a series of lamp posts and items of railway furniture. This was drawn originally on white paper with a black ball-point pen. The purpose of this drawing is to show the varieties of lamp posts, and of designs used by the various railway companies. Although not sketched on site, they have been developed into this form from field notes.

If a similar type of drawing is required for publication, the

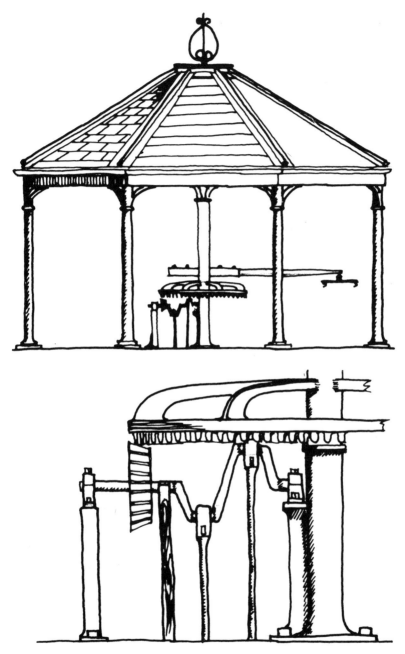

Fig 54. The horse wheel at Shabden Park near Croydon
(awaiting re-erection at Grey's Court near Henley)

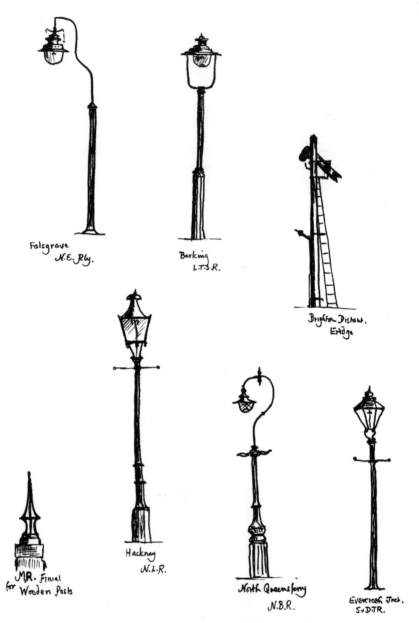

Falsgrave
N.E. Rly.

Barking
L.T.S.R.

Brighton Distant.
Eridge

M.R. Finial
for Wooden Posts

Hackney
N.L.R.

North Queensferry
N.B.R.

Evercreech Jnct.
S.D.J.R.

Fig 55. Sketches of lamp posts and signal posts by Lawrence
Cameron

fieldworker may wish to produce a better line drawing. For this he should use 'rapidograph' type pens with Indian ink, tracing paper and a drawing board. The 'Quickdraw' shown in Figure 41 is drawing board with loose T-square, set-square and adjustable one of the boards which can be used. The more conventional set-square is often used, but this is essentially a method to be used at home.

If a fieldworker needs to illustrate an item of equipment or a building in a publication which is unable to be illustrated with blocks because of expense, then it is possible to produce an acceptable drawing by tracing over a projected colour slide or a black and white photograph, using black ink on good quality draughtsman's tracing paper. The worker must also think of the size of the finished product, and make allowances if the finished page is to be a reduction in size of the original. If, for example, the reduction is two times, lines must be twice as thick as those of the finished product.

PHOTOGRAPHS

The intention of this section is to give the industrial archaeologist some practical help with photography. When the industrial archaeologist begins to take part in serious fieldwork he will soon find that a camera is indispensable. The rate of demolition of industrial monuments and machinery is so high that a photograph taken by a newcomer to the subject may well be the last ever taken of a particular building or process or piece of machinery. A photograph may be the only record which remains to show future historians, economists or engineers what certain types of plant were like, or how a particular local industry was housed.

As colour film is still liable to fade or change because it is based on dyes, a photographic record should always be made on black and white film. Coloured slides or prints can be useful as lecture material, but the use of colour should be secondary to the industrial archaeologist's black and white record photographs. Many copies can be taken off a negative quite easily, and a good print in black and white with high contrast can be used as the basis of any publication where blocks are going to be made. When photographs are being deliberately taken to form the sole record of an industrial monument, the industrial archaeologist must plan his photographs carefully so that they show the salient features of both exterior and interior, and in so doing identify the various items of equipment in relation to the spaces they occupy. Vital parts of a building should be photographed as separate items, and related to the whole complex in general arrangement photographs.

If the industrial archaeologist is preparing measured drawings in addition to a photographic record, he should feel no qualms of conscience in using his camera as a second 'notebook' to give additional information and to fill in details. Measured drawings can be complemented by photographs of elevations taken squarely, and by elevation photographs of machinery.

Photographs which are going to be used for publication should be of a very high quality. A check should be made with the publisher to find out if the selection of prints is adequate, and before the blocks are made, new prints should be obtained which meet the high standards of the block-maker. These prints should, ideally, be prepared to the size of the intended block; in this way there is less loss of detail in the printed picture.

As the industrial archaeologist gets deeper into his subject, he will discover an increasing dependence on photography. He will also want to discuss his 'finds' with members of his own group, or with other enthusiasts at conferences or meetings. It is useful to have an album of photographs on these occasions, and also to have selected colour slides of particular interests. At conferences or meetings there are often screens on which current work can be displayed, or members may be invited to show colour slides of recent or interesting discoveries. For lecture purposes, slides can be in colour, or can be black and white positives made from 35 mm negatives.

The choice of a camera will largely depend on the state of the industrial archaeologist's finances. The idealist will claim, quite rightly, that the best photographs are those taken by the older type of plate camera with interchangeable lenses, rising and cross front. However, this involves the photographer in carrying heavy equipment, and he can spend a long time on site taking photographs. Probably the best alternative is the Rolleiflex type of twin lens reflex camera, but the disadvantage of this system is the inability to change lenses. The amateur will more frequently opt for a 35 mm camera, and the many models on the market offer a wide range of alternatives. Another useful camera would be the type of through-the-lens reflex which can take interchangeable lenses, and which has flash contacts and a reasonable range of focal stops, speeds, and some kind of long time exposure. There are many models which satisfy these basic requirements in the £20 to £30 range. Only after considerable experience will the industrial archaeologist feel that a more sophisticated camera is necessary.

Having invested in a camera, the industrial archaeologist will also need to add various other items of equipment to this as time goes on. For black and white, but obviously not for colour work, a yellow filter which pushes over the lens is invaluable. When used out of doors it renders clouds correctly in a sky which would otherwise remain blank, and heightens the contrast in shadows. Using a filter doubles the length of exposure, or can increase it even more according to the filter's factor. If the industrial archaeologist is engaged in fieldwork at various times of the day throughout the year, he will also need an exposure meter. Since he will also wish to take interior photographs, and possibly colour shots on a second camera, an independent light meter is more reliable than one coupled into the camera. For interior work and also for good flash photographs taken outside, the industrial archaeologist should have a good form of tripod. If a great amount of fieldwork is being undertaken, investment in an electronic flash gun will prove a useful saving in time, and used properly, will enable more complete records to be made even in the darkest interiors.

The use of interchangeable lenses has been discussed in considering the purchase of a camera. The second lens which the industrial archaeologist will require will be a wide-angle lens. When working outside, the photographer is rarely limited in the distance he needs to step back in order to include the whole of his subject, but when photographing a crowded interior, such as the stone-floor of a corn-mill, he is unable to take in the whole area without a wide-angle lens. The focal length of such a lens should be about 30 mm to 35 mm for a standard 35 mm camera format. With a shorter focal length the cost of the lens becomes greater, and has the added disadvantage of distorting the subject. The normal focal length of the 35 mm camera is 50 mm. Although a telephoto lens is useful, its use is so infrequent that it should be one of the last items of equipment purchased.

The industrial archaeologist is now frequently faced with the need to copy old drawings, photographs and records to make his study of a subject complete. The editor uses a system based on a tripod with a reversible column and two equally powered table-lamps. Whilst larger documents can be copied using the standard lens, the copying of postcards and small objects will need either extension tubes or 'proxar' lenses which push over the standard lens like a filter. It is important to remember that extension tubes alter the exposure according to their factor, but that 'proxar' lenses do not. The two lamps should be set so that they illuminate the subject equally from either side.

General views should be taken in such a way that the vertical lines do not converge because the camera was tilted. If a building is in strong sunlight with really deep shadows then a compromise exposure should be made so that the shadow is not so black that the detail is obscured. When taking an exposure meter reading the meter should be pointed at a building rather than at the sky to give a more correct exposure for the building. The photographs by Eric de Maré in the book *The Functional Tradition* should be studied, for there the record photographs have a quality equal to that of art photographs, and show how one can get away from the straight elevation type of photograph and the 'picture postcard' effect.

When one is using a tripod interiors are not difficult to photograph, but one must be careful to avoid photographs which include a direct view of a window as an unbalanced exposure causes 'flare' and can give the pattern of the iris of the lens on the negative. If the range of light in the interior is great, the time exposure should be geared to compromise between bright areas and darker shadows. Sometimes experienced photographers will take a time exposure and then release a flash gun on open flash in various parts of a room to light as much of the area as possible to a standard level. With a flash gun there are several disadvantages which can be overcome by careful use. The worst feature is that the flash gun is mounted on the camera and therefore causes an object to be illuminated without any shadows, producing a dead flat picture. An extension lead should be used to place the flash gun to the left or right of the camera to give some modelling and shadows. The range of most flash guns in the amateur's price bracket will give reasonable illumination up to a maximum distance of about 15 ft. To get a greater range the stop of the lens has to be reduced to such a level that there is little depth of field in the picture. If a greater depth of field is required, then a multiple flash exposure, with the camera on a tripod as described above, should be used.

The criterion for photographs for publication is a strong contrasting print with needle-sharp focus. Here, your publisher should give you assistance by indicating from proof prints of your photographs what his requirements are.

Many local industrial archaeology groups or local history societies are now publishing newsletters or bulletins. For publications with a small circulation the Xerox type of reproduction can be used. For this system the cost of photographic blocks is prohibitive, and the production of a drawing by tracing over a photograph on tracing paper with Indian ink is an acceptable solution. The resultant page, if the same size as the typescript, can be stapled up with the newsletter.

Fig 56. Cast-iron plate on stone milepost on Thomas Telford's Holyhead Road, now the A5. Drawn from a black and white photograph

Whilst photography is not something of which to be afraid, the industrial archaeologist should try out all his equipment before using it for serious fieldwork, so that the operation of the camera and various pieces of equipment becomes automatic. When doing fieldwork, one should work on the assumption that one might not have the opportunity to go back if one has omitted something or not connected the flash gun in the right way!

THE NATIONAL RECORD OF INDUSTRIAL MONUMENTS

When the discipline of Industrial Archaeology was detailed in the first edition of this book, references to the National Record of Industrial Monuments were left out. This was basically because the National Record of Industrial Monuments (NRIM) had only just begun to receive information from workers in the field and was not an established institution. Six years later it is an accepted part of the discipline, and its growth over the six years justifies a description of its function being included in this edition.

The record card around which the NRIM is built was introduced by the Council for British Archaeology after it had set up the Research Committee for Industrial Archaeology in 1959. The National Survey of Industrial Monuments, with its first Consultant on Industrial Monuments, Mr Rex Wailes, was brought into being and it received the record cards to help the Consultant to identify sites in areas in which he was working. The patchiness of the records made at this stage did not contribute greatly towards the work of the Consultant in any given area. He was, in fact, forced to do the local fieldwork himself, assisted by people whom he knew in the various localities.

When the concern for a preservation policy for industrial monuments was being presented to the then Minister of Public Building and Works, it was decided to process the record cards differently, and to make the material more readily available to users. At that time, the Director of the Centre for the Study of the History of Technology at the University of Bath, Dr R. A. Buchanan, took over the responsibility for processing the cards. These are copied and then returned to the worker by Dr Buchanan; a copy is retained at the University of Bath where it can be consulted; a copy is sent to the

National Monuments Record in London where it can also be consulted; and a further copy is given to the CBA Consultant on Industrial Archaeology.

It is hoped that NRIM can eventually be used as a guide to preservation policy for industrial monuments, but at present only Hertfordshire has received the sort of concentrated recording which would enable a county's policy to be formulated from record cards. To this end, the cards are standardized, and can be punched in such a way that they can be used on a punched-card system, although the number of cards completed and the inadequacy of the coverage would make the effort of punching rather pointless. There are only some 6,000 cards in the records at the moment for all forms of industrial site, and it is estimated that there are 10,000 watermill and 3,000 windmill sites in this country, so one gains an idea of the paucity of the present state of NRIM.

It is hoped that as many fieldworkers as possible can help to remedy the lack of records of industrial monuments. The record cards are invaluable for seeing the whole range of industrial sites for a given subject, or for assessing the processes of geographical change which have taken place in an industry. In the long term, the records will assist the study of economic history and geography, and the identification of all sites of an industry in a particular area.

The cards for NRIM can be obtained from The Council for British Archaeology, 8 St Andrews Place, Regents Park, London NW1. The following notes constitute a few simple rules for filling in cards:

(i) The cards should be typed or written legibly in a black or dark ink as pencil and light blue ink do not copy on standard Xerox copiers. A normal longhand script tends to blur and become unreadable when copied.

(ii) Give grid references clearly and accurately. These should be in the form shown on the bottom of 1 in Ordnance Survey maps, i.e. with two letters and six figures (e.g. Morwellham Quay SX 445 695).

(iii) In filling in the 'Nature of Site' panel it is useful to put more than just 'copper mine'; the name of the mine should be added where known, e.g. 'Devon Great Consols Copper Mine'.

(iv) It is important to fill in the county and the parish correctly for these are essential if the cards are to be compared with the lists of buildings of special architectural or historical interest prepared under the provisions of the Planning Acts.

(v) The reference number panel is not to be filled in before despatch, as this is filled by the classification number used by Bath University.

(vi) Date of report. This is important, for when the card is used to determine what is happening to a site, the latest report can be identified.

(vii) The face of the card should be filled with the recorder's description of the monument, its various parts, and the recorder's knowledge of any threat under which the monument is known to be.

(viii) The panel for Danger of Demolition or Damage should be left blank if this is not known.

(ix) Printed, Manuscript or Photographic Records. This should contain the recorder's knowledge of how far the monument has been detailed in local records, and should also note if the recorder has taken measurements and photographed the monument.

(x) The back of the card should be used for further notes or for a descriptive sketch with rough dimensions. Photographs should not be fastened to the card as these do not copy on Xerox machines.

The record card should be completed as one of the first jobs of the fieldworker on his return home or to his hotel. (Professor Sir Nikolaus Pevsner, when compiling his *Buildings of England* series, writes up each day's finds that same evening.) The purpose of the card is to record the existence of an industrial monument and its

NATURE OF SITE (Factory, mine, etc.)
WIND PUMP & CORN MILL

COUNTY
HAMPSHIRE.

REF. No.

GRID REFERENCE OR LOCATION.
SU 427 564.

INDUSTRY.
WATER RAISING & CORN MILLING.

DATING.
1892

PARISH/TOWNSHIP.
CRUX EASTON

DATE OF REPORT.
1 - 7 - 1972

DESCRIPTION: dimensions; present condition; architectural features etc. A 'SIMPLEX' WINDMILL BY
JOHN WALLIS TITT OF WARMINSTER BUILT 1892. 36' HIGH HEXAGONAL STEEL
LATTICE TOWER. 3'-9" FACES TO CAST IRON BASE PLATE. BRICK MILL BUILDING
CONTAINING WELL ON LOWER FLOOR c1700 STILL STANDING ADJACENT.
40 CANVAS COVERED SAILS IN 24' DIAMETER WHEEL. (SAILS DELIBERATELY
REMOVED) 8 SPOKES. 6 BLADED FAN TAIL TO TURN MILL INTO WIND. BALANCE
BLOCKS ON FAN BEAMS. GEAR REMOVED FROM BASE & MILL.
(Further remarks or photo/sketch may be recorded on the back) (8/10 SACKS GROUND PER DAY).

MACHINERY AND FITTINGS. NIL. REMOVED.

DANGER OF DEMOLITION OR DAMAGE.

PRINTED, MANUSCRIPT OR PHOTOGRAPHIC RECORDS. PHOTOS J.K.M.
CAT. 1911 OF J.WALLIS TITT OF WARMINSTER CARRIES TESTIMONIALS OF 1892 & 1894
FOR THIS MACHINE.

REPORTER'S NAME AND ADDRESS:- J. KENNETH MAJOR
2 ELDON ROAD
READING
RG1 4DH.

Return to:-
J.K.MAJOR

INSTITUTION OR SOCIETY:-

LOVER.

C.B.A. INDUSTRIAL ARCHAEOLOGY REPORT CARD.

Fig 57. The record card for the wind engine at Crux Easton,
Hampshire

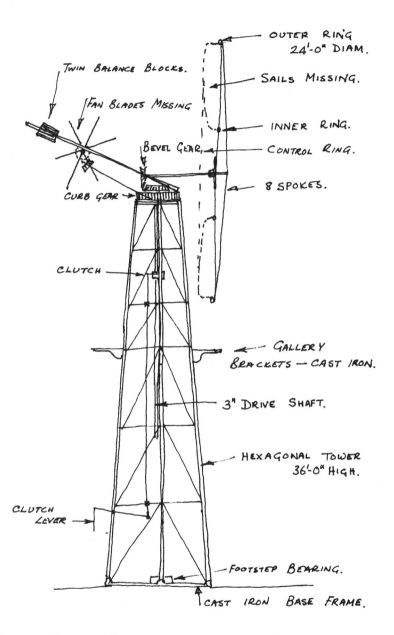

OUTER RING
24'-0" DIAM.

SAILS MISSING.

TWIN BALANCE BLOCKS.

FAN BLADES MISSING

INNER RING.

BEVEL GEAR.

CONTROL RING.

CURB GEAR

8 SPOKES.

CLUTCH

GALLERY
BRACKETS — CAST IRON.

3" DRIVE SHAFT.

HEXAGONAL TOWER
36'-0" HIGH.

CLUTCH
LEVER

FOOTSTEP BEARING.

CAST IRON BASE FRAME.

CRUX EASTON, HAMPSHIRE.

Fig 58. The reverse face of the record card for the wind engine
at Crux Easton, Hampshire

Fig 59. The state of industrial buildings for recording

state of repair. Its completion should not be held up until the worker has examined every document in the local record office to produce an 'Old Testament' list of owners or managers down the centuries.

Figures 57 and 58 show a typical record card, in this case the wind engine at Crux Easton in Hampshire. This wind engine was found five hours after seeing a testimonial to its maker in his catalogue for 1911, and the record card was filled in that night.

To assist in the assessment of the state of an industrial building, Figure 59 has been drawn at the suggestion of Douglas Hague. This classification is useful, and the recorder should not be afraid to send in a card for items which are ruins or sites only, for in this way the total pattern of an industry can be built up.

I hope that the fieldworker will take this chapter to heart, for it is only by achieving a complete record that we will be able to pursue preservation of our industrial monuments on a sensible scale in the immediate future.

CHAPTER SEVEN

The Scope of Industrial Archaeology

THE industrial archaeologist is often bewildered by the scale of the subject which is presented to him when he first enters the discipline. In actual fact, the scale is no greater than that of the discipline of the medieval archaeologist or the classical archaeologist. This chapter aims to present some, but by no means all, of the guidelines for workers in the discipline.

The authors who first laid down these guidelines in the early 1960s chose broad headings: 1 Coal and Metals, 2 Power, 3 Textiles, Pottery and Glass, Brewing and Distilling, 4 Transport, 5 Building Materials, 6 Agricultural Industry. Since that period further items for study have come to be accepted as part of the discipline: 7 Housing for Industrial Workers, 8 Public Services, 9 Industry of Recreation. Although a great deal of discussion still takes place over the true scope of the discipline, the industrial archaeologist who does not work at the subject on a full-time basis will be able to adjust his personal range to suit his interests. Many of the facets of a particular element of the study are without records or documents and it is often the discovery of these incidental items which can give the greatest joy and contribute to the extension of our knowledge of the subject.

Whilst the general starting point for the subject covered by the broad term 'industrial archaeology' can be thought to be the middle of the eighteenth century, many innovations and improvements in manufacturing processes or in transport started before that date. Some industrial archaeologists would claim that the stone axe factory on Stickle Pike in Westmorland, which dates from about 1500 BC, falls within their concern as it certainly had an element of mass production and was used for trade because the axes were exported all over the British Isles. Others hold that the study of the use of the waterwheel for power must begin in the Roman period, and, in the case of the horizontal waterwheel, even earlier and further east than that. However, the industrial archaeologist will temper his own personal views with the needs of his chosen subject or the area in which he is working. The end of the period of study is usually taken as the end of the nineteenth century or the start of World War I. Again, this is clearly too limiting, for many processes which now form part of our industrial past did not start until after those dates. The rate at which processes become obsolete means that industrial plant which was built only a few years ago has now been abandoned. An example of this is seen in those gas works which lost their conventional retort houses (where coal was turned into gas and coke) when naphtha conversion plants were built about 1960, and which are now losing this plant on the introduction of natural gas.

In considering the study of the subject the broad headings given as guidelines at the beginning of this chapter can be broken down further to give some hint of the pattern which should be followed in examining the remains and documents of a particular industry.

COAL AND METALS

Whilst the mining of coal and the various metals, iron, lead, copper and tin goes back to the period of pre-Roman studies, the real remains of those mining industries appear from the medieval era onwards. Bell-pits for the mining of coal and iron are sometimes found during open-cast mining for those minerals. The bell-pits at Bentley Grange, Elmley, Yorkshire, are an example of an intense mining industry carried on by Byland Abbey, one of the Cistercian monasteries. The remains of hush mining for lead can be seen in the Mendips and the Pennines. This medieval method consisted of eroding the ore out of a vein by a large force of water released when an artificial reservoir was breached at the head of the vein. Deep mining for copper by the German mine engineers imported by the Mines Royal about 1560 can be seen in Simon's Nick in the Coniston massif in the Furness area of Lancashire.

Later methods of coal mining can be studied in all the coalfields where mines can often be found abandoned and replaced by later types. Pithead gears for raising the coal and the miners from the bottom of shafts remain in quite a few places, though the search for recoverable scrap means that these steel head-gears are often sold soon after the closure of the mine. Again, the change from steam engine winding to electric hoists meant that the form of the pithead gear changed. Because of the lighter weight of the hoist motors and winding drums the modern pithead gear is housed in a concrete room on top of a concrete tower. Coal separation plants have not changed very much; the buildings are possibly more substantial now, and no longer made of rusty corrugated iron as they were in the early part of this century. On the social side, there are the bath houses and canteens which were built in collieries in the 1930s and which followed to a certain extent the brick designs of the Dutch architect Dudok. With the introduction of bathrooms in the poorer housing in the pit villages and the rise in ownership of the motor car these buildings are becoming redundant.

The disposal of waste after the extraction of coal leads to considerable variation in method with consequent differences in the industrial landscape. Some mines can run railways out horizontally over a valley and tip at the end of each run; others run a tipper truck up an incline and tip off the top producing an ever-growing cone. In some areas the waste is tipped from tubs on aerial ropeways, producing a level tip with pimples under the tipping points.

The industrial remains of metal mining are usually less complete, for there is now hardly any metal extraction in Britain, except open-cast working for iron in the Midlands. In the mountainous districts of Cumbria, Wales and Cornwall there are the remains of lead, copper and tin mining. In these areas the industrial archaeologist can find a great deal to interest him as well as giving him a holiday in good country. There are often large sites with lots of surface works, water courses, reservoirs, waterwheel sites and crushing plants, with debris from both the mines and the ore-crushing plants everywhere. In Robert Clough's book *Lead Smelting Mills of the Yorkshire Dales* you can see that even though the industry has been worked out for a long time, there are a great number of remains which can be studied so that the pattern of an industrial process can be determined from them. In the Coppermines Valley of the Coniston massif there are four different smelt mill sites which followed each other, and the various stages in their growth and abandonment can be discerned by the keen industrial archaeologist.

The tin mining field can offer far more positive remains than the copper and lead mining fields of the north of England. In Cornwall there was considerable tin mining activity up to the first quarter of this century, and as the mines were deep, there was a great deal of water to be pumped out, so there were hundreds of engines in their characteristic engine-houses all over the peninsula. Some engines have been preserved, but the engine-houses provide an exciting study themselves. There are numerous remains; washing plants, water-driven crushing plants, railways and spoil heaps, which exist to tell us more about the Cornish tin industry and its working methods.

The remains of ore processing in the areas where lead, copper and tin were mined rarely contain complete buildings, and most frequently are so ruinous as to need conventional archaeological excavation techniques to determine their form. In the field of iron processing the remains are much more abundant though they are often in remote areas. Early blast furnaces for the production of pig iron from high grade iron ore still exist in the Furness district of Lancashire, in Shropshire, and in Scotland. The furnace on the Cumberland bank of the river Duddon at Duddon Bridge shows the whole range of work on a site of the early eighteenth century.

There are storage houses, charcoal houses, the furnace itself, the tuyeres and the waterwheels which drove the blowing engines. There is also the manager's house together with some cottages and an office block with cart sheds and stabling. Similar complexes remain in the Forest of Dean and at Bonawe and Furnace in Scotland. A rather late series exists in the Ironbridge Gorge Museum complex. Later examples of blast furnaces can be seen up and down the country, but the areas where iron is still made are going over to modern highly mechanized methods, and so the late nineteenth-century plant is being demolished. Wellingborough, Northamptonshire, now has none of its sculptured blast furances, and its iron-making sites have all been erased and replaced by a modern industrial estate.

POWER

The production of power in its various forms probably attracts most industrial archaeologists to the subject in the first place. There is a vast range of material here for study. The natural forms of power spring most readily to mind. Waterwheels are perhaps the most numerous of the remains of natural power sources. Apart from the study of the wheels themselves, there is the associated problem of the supply of water to provide the most efficient working for a given situation. There are also the various types of wheel construction which have an historical significance. If one takes the horizontal waterwheel as an earlier and now separate type, the waterwheel can vary between the simple stream wheel and the great 'engineered' wheels such as those of Casement, Donkin and Sir William Fairburn. There are enough remaining of the whole range to make their study very rewarding.

The windmill is now becoming rarer, except where it has been deliberately preserved. The historical study of the technology of the windmill is by no means complete, although there have been good books produced in recent years. *The English Windmill* by

Plate 7. Tide mill at Eling, Hampshire

Plate 8. General view of the first floor at Eling Mill

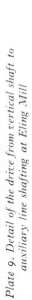

Plate 10. Point of an oak pile drawn from the mud at Southampton in 1949. The point was hewn with an axe, the marks still showing, and then charred. This pile had probably been in the sea bed

Plate 9. Detail of the drive from vertical shaft to auxiliary line shafting at Eling Mill

Rex Wailes is the most comprehensive study. Attention is now being drawn to the need to study wind engines—those circular-sailed windmills made of galvanized iron and mounted on latticed steel towers and used for pumping water, generating electricity, or, in some cases, for grinding corn. Even a modern product such as this can have a great many variations of design.

Animal engines, that is machines which turn the tractive effort of a beast into rotary motion, are turning up for study in many places. Perhaps the most numerous examples of these are in the horse wheel or gin-gang, attached to farms to carry out a multitude of jobs like threshing, chaff-cutting, oat-crushing and meal-grinding. Eight hundred sites of these have been listed in the north of England alone. The cider crusher and apple-crushing machines still exist in the west of England. Clay mills and pug mills driven by horses can still be found in some primitive brick-yards. The work of the horse and donkey in contributing to the supply of water is detailed in Brunner and Major's *Water Raising by Animal Power* which appeared in *Industrial Archaeology* vol 9, no 2.

Steam power excites most industrial archaeologists. The first introduction of steam for pumping water from mines dates from the second quarter of the eighteenth century, and reached its greatest heights of efficiency in the first quarter of the twentieth century when steam engines were used to drive almost everything. The work of Newcomen and the other engine inventors does not need to be enlarged on. The study of the remaining engines does. Not all engines can or should be preserved, but they should all be fully recorded. The gradual development from the Newcomen engine through the engines of Boulton and Watt, the Cornish engines and the large compound engines in water works and cotton mills is being pieced together slowly. There has as yet been no systematic study made of existing engines which once supplied water to the various communities up and down the country. A further element of this is the necessary study of the boiler systems which supplied the steam to these engines; of the buildings which housed them, and of their chimneys. *The Stationary Steam Engine* and *The Textile Mill Engine* by George Watkins together with D. Bradford Barton's *The Cornish Beam Engine* do set out the types and development of small areas of industrial steam power. Diesel, gas, electricity and atomic power have now virtually supplanted the steam engine, and even these fields now contain historic examples which have passed into the range of industrial archaeology.

MANUFACTURING INDUSTRIES

Perhaps the greatest range of industrial remains occurs in the area of the manufacturing industries. Throughout Britain there are areas devoted to particular manufacturing processes; cotton spinning in south Lancashire, cotton weaving in mid-Lancashire, woollen processing in Yorkshire, and pottery in Staffordshire. The areas where these occur contain the whole range of the processes, with modern mills standing cheek by jowl with earlier examples. In other places the early factories are all that remain. An example of this is the woollen industry in the Golden Valley around Stroud where the industry has now died out.

The textile industry provides us with some of our finest industrial buildings, e.g. the Georgian woollen mills and miller's house at Chalford, upstream from Stroud in the Golden Valley; the Arkwright mill buildings of the Derwent valley south of Matlock, and in Cromford; the silk mills of Derby and Macclesfield; and fireproof structures in multi-storey industrial buildings as shown by those mills at Belper in Derbyshire erected by William Strutt in the 1790s. All these early mills had interesting power systems. Great waterwheels such as those at Calva Mill in Derbyshire and at Lothersdale pre-dated the introduction of steam engines. The waterwheels or steam engines were connected to lay shafts which ran the whole length of each floor, and from these lay shafts the individual machines, whether spinning frames or looms, were driven.

Textiles started as an industry in the home, and all over the country specially designed houses still exist which provided workrooms for these cottage industries. The silk workers' houses in Spitalfields in the East End of London are an example of these, and they are distinguished by the larger range of windows provided to give better light in the workrooms.

As well as the processing of the raw materials into textiles, there are the various warehouses where the raw materials and finished goods were stored, and the Exchange buildings where cotton and wool were bought and sold. Associated industrial processes are also important, and bleach works and dye houses which still remain form part of the industry's history.

In those areas where flax and linen were produced there are industrial remains peculiar to those processes. The flax was reduced to its constituent fibres in beetling mills where water-powered hammers beat the flax after it had partially rotted in water. From the beetling mills the fibres went to be spun into linen yarn and then woven. Associated with the weaving sheds there were large fields where the new linen cloth was laid out to bleach in the sun. Because of the risk of theft, there were small watch-houses built in these fields.

Paper has been made in Britain for a very long time, and the remains of the industry can be seen by many of our rivers. Water was needed to power the mills, and clean water was required during manufacture. The industry's remains are often quite distinctive as the process requires definite stages during manufacture. On papermaking sites there are usually barns for the storage of the rags which were used. The actual mill needed a waterwheel to power the rag-breakers, the hammers and the hollanders, but most of the other parts of the older processes were carried out by hand. A typical stuff mill (a mill where the basic fibre is produced from rags) was the little mill which stood at Slaughterford in Wiltshire some distance above the present paper mill. Here a watercourse about half a mile long brought water to a 15 ft diameter high breast shot waterwheel. This waterwheel powered the mill by means of a lay shaft driven by a rim gear on the waterwheel. Process steam was provided by a Lancashire boiler on the upstream side of the mill. The steam was circulated with the necessary alkaline solution in two rag-boilers. The rags were cut by special machines before being put into the breaking engines. Special elm-bodied trucks were used to carry the wet 'stuff' to the lower mill. Another characteristic on paper mill sites is a drying shed which had adjustable openings in the walls, and which may still have the hooks on either side from which cow-hair ropes were stretched on which the individual sheets of paper were hung to dry. At the beginning of the nineteenth century continuous paper-making machines were brought into use, and factories which use this type of machine for making paper still exist today, though, of course, in a modern form.

Pottery has played a large part in our industrial history as it provided much of the impetus behind the creation of the early canal system in Staffordshire, Cheshire and south Lancashire. Materials, coal, china clay and flint, had to be brought from the coalfields or from the port of Liverpool to the Potteries. The characteristic form of the pottery (clay sheds, drying sheds, painters' studios, and bottle kilns) can no longer be seen. The Five Towns which form the Potteries no longer have hundreds of belching kilns. The whole process is cleaner now as the firing no longer needs coal, but can be better controlled using gas or electricity. This means that the traditional form is lost, and a prosaic factory is now standard for pottery production.

The associated elements of the pottery trade, the stone-grinding mills and the china clay pits of Cornwall, are very much part of the industrial scene, and, although the china clay pits are still extremely active in Cornwall and Devon, the water-driven stone-grinding mills are no longer in use. However, examples are preserved at Cheddleton in Staffordshire and at Tregargus in the St Stephen Valley in Cornwall.

Glass making was carried on all over England at one time, but has now come to be associated with only one town, St Helens, and one company, Pilkingtons. The remains of early glass works are quite distinctive where they survive, for the works were created around the glass cone. This large cone made of stone or brick was the place which contained not only the furnaces for producing the liquid glass, but also the area where the men actually blew the glass and produced the glass products, i.e. crown glass for windows, wineglasses, beakers, and all manner of blown ware. Glass cones still exist, but not in use, at Bristol, Leamington-on-Tyne, and Catcliff near Sheffield. Polished window glass came in about 1800 when the use of steam engines became universal. These could be used to provide power for beds which ground and polished the glass after it had been cast on an iron table. The present production of glass bears no resemblance to the earlier forms of glass making, as it is now a continuous process, with the molten glass being drawn out of the molten tanks or being drawn horizontally over heated tables.

Food processing has not been an industrial process for very long, for until the twentieth century almost everything was made at home or no further away than the shop on the corner. It was not until the invention of refrigeration that meat or dairy products could be produced in large quantities for export. At about the same time, the packing of food in hermetically sealed cans became possible, and a whole series of factories grew up to serve the new industry. Dairies were built in the country in areas served by the railways so that an overnight delivery of milk could take place to London and the larger cities. In fruit-growing areas fruit-canning and jam-making factories were started. In the immediate environs of London and some large cities there was a big market-gardening industry with large acreages under glass, where fruit, vegetables and flowers were produced

on a commercial scale. At the receiving end of the food production
cycle there was a whole industry devoted to marketing the produce
and London's great central markets, Smithfield (meat), Billingsgate
(fish), and Covent Garden (fruit and vegetables), to name but a few,
were built. Marketing methods and changes in transport have meant
that even these markets have come to the end of their usefulness.
For example, frozen fish has meant a complete change from the
traditional method of marketing fish.

Brewing has a distinctive industrial pattern and one can still find
breweries all over the country where nineteenth-century brewing
practice is still being carried on. The drawing of a brewery in
Rees' Cyclopedia shows the typical nineteenth-century brewery
which existed in our large towns. There are still small public house
and large estate brewhouses in existence, with their equipment,
which give us an idea of what these simpler breweries were like.
A good example of this type of brewery is the one recently gutted
behind the Wellington Arms, mid-way between Reading and
Basingstoke, which was the brewhouse of the Duke of Wellington's
Stratfield Saye estate. The process of mergers is now combining
the existing breweries, and many of them, on merging with larger
groups, cease to do any brewing and quickly lose their traditional
equipment.

Malting plays a large part in the brewing process, and traditional
buildings still exist in many places. These form exciting shapes well
worthy of study, and, in many instances, worthy of preservation.
The kilns, which can be square or circular, are attached to long
buildings which have small windows. In the long buildings germination of the barley takes place on each floor, the grain then has its
germination stopped in the kiln before being sent on to the brewery.
There are many maltings which exist separately as private firms, or
which are attached to mills and frequently to breweries. Hop
kilns, though not so large, form groups of similarly important shapes
in Kent, Hampshire and Herefordshire.

Perhaps the area of food processing most studied is the milling industry, and this is probably because the remains are so widespread. Almost everywhere one goes in the British Isles there are windmills and watermills for grinding corn. Although the majority of watermills have mid-nineteenth-century milling and power systems, there is a vast range of technical history to be discovered in others which have wooden gearing systems dating from the early eighteenth century. Others show the highly productive milling systems of the end of the nineteenth century when roller milling, as opposed to grinding between stones, was firmly established. In windmills there is a complete range of historical technical survival in the remains which are to be seen throughout Britain.

TRANSPORT

The road pattern of this country was formed in very early times, but it is the remains of the turnpike roads which were constructed during the eighteenth century that are of significance for the industrial archaeologist. The Turnpike Age is shown very well in the milestones, finger posts and toll houses; in some instances the pumps used for watering the horses and keeping down the dust still remain. Occasional stretches of original turnpike roads remain where they have been bypassed by later alignments, or where they were overlaid with later construction without alteration to their function.

The modern road has many industrial remains which date from the introduction of the motor car. These remains, traffic signs and signals, petrol pumps and garages, are well worthy of serious study.

Rivers have been used for transport from the Middle Ages, but works of navigation, flash locks, pound locks and cuts, did not come into being until the seventeenth and eighteenth centuries. A navigation such as the Kennet up to Newbury from Reading, shows quite a lot of its pre-1810 form, and there are turf-sided locks, which, though renewed many times, pre-date Rennie's construction of the Kennet and Avon Canal. The true canal period started with the works of the Duke of Bridgewater connecting his mines at Worsley in south Lancashire with Salford and Manchester in 1759. Brindley, who was the constructor of the Duke of Bridgewater's canals, went on to construct other canals which were promoted by many different companies and which stretched across the face of England from the Lancaster Canal, which went from Preston to Kendal, to the Andover and Salisbury Canals which were intended to connect those towns to Southampton Water. Canal construction ceased in the 1850s with the building of the last inland canal, the Hereford and Gloucester. Over the one hundred years of active canal construction many interesting canals were built, and their construction contains many of the great monuments of the industrial revolution, such as Pont Cysyllte aqueduct, the Devizes and Tardebigge flights of locks, the Foxton inclined plane, and the Anderton lift. For the industrial archaeologist there is a great deal to discover on the canal system whether it is live, like the Grand Junction Canal, or very dead, like the Andover or the North Walsham and Dilham Canals.

More enthusiasts concentrate on railways and their history than on any other form of industrial monument, but very few of them would count themselves industrial archaeologists, for their concern lies with the preservation of the visible and live remains of their industry. For the industrial archaeologist there is a very definite pre-history of railways going back well into the eighteenth century. These lost lines, usually built to serve industry in some way, can form interesting studies and often provide unexpected finds for the industrial archaeologist. There has been a great deal of historical and descriptive writing concerned with railways, from George Stephenson's time down to the present day, and the bibliography of railways is being extended all the time. Much of the industrial archaeology has been left untouched. Work needs to be done, for instance, on the design of railway stations and the reasons behind certain plan forms and decorative treatments. Little or nothing has been done on the standardization of railway buildings proposed by Brunel, Brassey, and other contemporary engineers.

All the preceding studies under the heading 'transport' need bridges, and whilst there is a great deal of information on the contribution made by the great engineers to the history of bridge building, there are hundreds of bridge structures up and down the country which have made significant contributions to the history of bridge building. Sir John Vanbrugh's bridge at Blenheim, the Skerton bridge at Lancaster built in 1783, Robert Stephenson's High Level Bridge at Newcastle dated 1848, and Brunel's Windsor Bridge of 1849 are examples of these. Stone bridges of earlier periods are equally important, e.g. Twizel Bridge, Northumberland, the Devil's Bridge, Kirkby Lonsdale, and Framwellgate and Elvet Bridges in Durham City. These are a direct link between the earliest Roman structures and the great bridges of Rennie and Mylne, and, indeed, the present concrete bridges which are now being built.

There are several important types of building associated with transport. Warehouses are needed at all types of transportation points. The great warehouses of St Katherine's docks in London, and the warehouses of the Gloucester and Sharpness Canal at Gloucester are examples of architecturally pleasing structures, and at the other end of the scale one gets the small warehouse and stable blocks at the North Walsham wharf on the North Walsham and Dilham Canal. Now, of course, with fork-lift trucks for loading and unloading, warehouses have of necessity become single-storey buildings with lightweight cladding and simple steel-framed structures. Office blocks and station hotels often mask the pure engineering of the train sheds at big stations. These are just as much part of the railway scene as the tracks and signals.

The aircraft industry is one which tends to be overlooked. However, there are lots of early airports still in existence; aerodromes such as those described in the early novels of Neville Shute. The manufacturing plants on such aerodromes still exist, and again the office blocks, control towers and runway layouts still form significant remains on old airport sites. The old Croydon and Hendon airports have now been erased under housing and other developments, but there are little airports with their ancillary buildings in quite unexpected places, such as Ryde on the Isle of Wight, and these go back to the 'canvas and wire' days of the industry.

<h2>BUILDING MATERIALS</h2>

The natural materials which have been exploited for use in building construction have left many tangible remains behind. The medieval stonemasons used stone from Barnack near Peterborough for much of the Cambridge colleges, and for nearby churches. West of Barnack church there are several fields which can now support only scrub and weeds; these were the quarries. Quarries for stone and slate, and mines for Cotswold slates and Westmorland green slates still remain, and there is a great deal of industrial archaeology bound up in those remains. Perhaps the most dramatic of all the quarries are the slate quarries of North Wales and the quarry at Delabole in Cornwall. Associated with quarries there are many items of transport history such as the Haytor granite railway, the little railways of Wales, and typical ports such as Port Penrhyn near Bangor in north Wales.

There are substantial remains of the brick and tile industry, and a few works are still using the old methods of production. This helps the industrial archaeologist to read what he finds on old worked-out sites. Because of the substantial nature of the bricks in the kilns in the brickyards one can often find ranges of kilns when nothing else remains. The ranges of 'Newcastle' kilns at Belsay and Capheaton in Northumberland are examples of this. Even the great mechanized clay pits and brickyards of the Oxford clays are closing down, and there is a lot of interest in these. Many of the pits have large narrow-gauge railway systems or cable railways. The kilns are the large continuously burning type, and are surmounted by very tall chimneys which have often become curiously misshapen.

Concrete has come to replace brick and stone in modern building because it is not so 'labour intensive' as brick. To make concrete, gravel, sand and cement are required, and therefore large areas of gravel are dug up and the gravel is then taken away to building sites and motorways. The grading machines and delivery hoppers at the gravel pits can give quite dramatic sculptural effects, and their history is shown by the change in size of the machines with their rotating screens and steel hoppers. The actual production of cement requires large factories with tall chimneys to take the gritty smoke high so that it disperses more easily. There are early remains such as the old Medina Cement works near Newport, Isle of Wight, which was built as a tidal corn mill, and the early kilns in north Kent.

The timber industry is now nearly always an import business with no remains other than the slatted warehouses which occur at our ports or alongside some of our canals. Some large sawmills exist in timber-growing areas, but these are frequently only temporary buildings which can easily be rebuilt if the source of the timber changes. However, sawmills on estates such as that at Gunton Park in Norfolk, at Brightling Park in Sussex, and Tyninghame in East Lothian, show how wood sawing was carried on in the nineteenth century either by gang saws or circular saws.

AGRICULTURAL INDUSTRY

Apart from the factory processing of food, the agricultural industry has a lot of interesting remains which need to be sought out in various parts of the country. At quite an early date power was needed on farms to mechanize threshing and turnip chopping. In various parts of the country you can find farm waterwheels which drove all sorts of machines, in fact, some are known to have powered early milking machines. In the north, many farms had steam engines, and although these engines are no longer there, the chimneys remain. Horse engines were also used for threshing and other jobs, and in many cases the roundhouse which sheltered the horse and the machine still survives, although only rarely with the engine complete. Though not really part of the pattern of industrial archaeology, the planned farm estates and buildings of the nineteenth century are well worthy of study.

HOUSING FOR INDUSTRIAL WORKERS

When the workers first left their village houses and went to the towns they were crowded into slum dwellings, and their welfare was of no concern to the factory masters. However, the need to attract workers led to the creation of special housing estates adjacent to factories or works. The railway towns of Swindon in Wiltshire and Wolverton in Buckinghamshire both have small estates of workers' houses. Perhaps the best townships for workers were those which, in addition to being founded for need, were also built out of a sense of social improvement by the factory masters. Saltaire built by Sir Titus Salt and New Lanark built by Robert Owen are examples of such towns dating from the early part of the nineteenth century. In the twentieth century enlightened employers such as the Rowntrees, Cadburys and Levers, built industrial estates which were, in effect, garden cities, e.g. New Earswick at York, Bourneville near Birmingham, and Port Sunlight in the Wirral. Smaller units of good housing were associated with other industries. Stewartby in Bedfordshire and the cottages near the brickworks in Bletchley are examples of these. Though not strictly industrial, the estate workers' houses on some of the great estates were also model houses. Those at Alnwick on the Duke of Northumberland's estate, and in Basildon on the Basildon Park estate in Berkshire (built by Lutyens) are examples of these.

PUBLIC SERVICES

The public services can still provide us with some of our most dramatic monuments. Again, the present pattern of change will destroy many of these in the course of the next few years.

There are few large dams forming reservoirs in this country which are parallel to those in America or Africa. However, the dams at Vrynwy, Haweswater and Ladybower are fine examples of the smaller type of dam. The best monuments of the water-supply industry are the steam pumping stations which exist up and down the country to supply water to the larger towns. Many forms of steam engine are to be seen in these engine-houses, and some of them are of an incredible size. The Metropolitan Water Board's pumping plant at Walton-on-Thames is a cathedral of steam power. Some are now preserved, such as that at Ryhope near Sunderland, but many engine houses are being stripped to house diesel or electric motors. The London area with its seventeenth-century New River and its many pumping houses and reservoirs is an area well worthy of intensive study, in spite of the amount which has already been written about its water supply.

Gas works have now frequently been reduced to no more than a collection of gasholders with the associated valve houses. The production of gas from coal has ceased in all but two or three very remote stations in the north. Not all the retort houses of this period have been demolished, and they should be recorded before they are finally destroyed. Several gasholders are of very early date, and are frequently embellished with architectural features which make them objects of interest if not quite objects of beauty. Where natural gas is not yet available, gas is produced by the conversion of naphtha, and in these areas the gas works have been replaced by conversion plants which look like oil refineries on a smaller scale. The introduction of natural gas has made all gas production plant obsolete, and it is only a matter of time before it is all destroyed.

Electricity was produced in small power stations; almost one per town in the period up to World War II. This was largely because the electricity supply industry had grown up as a series of private or municipally owned companies. The power station at Newbury in Berkshire started off with two water turbine generators, to which were added two gas-driven generators (the gas being made behind the power station), then diesel engines, until at its close, in 1969, it had four huge diesel generators. At its close this power station was only on standby, but the engines could be switched on from Bristol! With the introduction of nationalization the industry became centralized, and one by one the smaller power stations have gone on standby, while others have gone out of use completely. The National Grid system means that fewer, but larger, power stations supply the total requirement of electric power. Large new power stations such as those at Fawley, Didcot and Drax, are fine buildings with big halls clad in glass and light cladding materials, and single tall multi-flued chimney stacks made of concrete. The earlier power stations were usually brick structures with several chimneys, and Battersea, and Ferrybridge in Yorkshire, are examples of these. The sculptured concrete cooling towers and wooden cooling towers are also worthy of study.

The postal and telegraph service is now being studied for it has a much neglected history. Quite a lot has been written about the ubiquitous pillar box, but not a lot about telephone kiosks. The exchange buildings of the telephone service have an architectural history from the very art-nouveau example at Reading, through the small country manual exchanges in their almost domestic buildings, to the large modern office block type of STD exchange. Postal sorting methods are changing all over Britain, and the postmen's offices with them. Bags are now carried on overhead railways through the offices, and no longer dragged along the floor. Electronic sorting takes place in some areas, and the laborious pigeon-hole type of sorting is no longer necessary. The other communication industries of radio and television also have an industrial history. Transmitters and radio stations have changed, and the old forest of masts is being replaced by the single high mast with several focused transmitters mounted on it. The use of old theatres and places of entertainment for studios and transmitting stations has not been studied. The television and radio industry grew faster than special buildings could be built to house it, and, with the exception of the national broadcasting buildings, a great many adapted buildings have been put into use and are still being used.

RECREATION INDUSTRY

A few people were surprised when the book *The Industrial Archaeology of the Isle of Man* appeared, because it analyses the hotel and boarding-house industry in some depth. This is not an unjustified inclusion in a book on industrial archaeology, as a great many people on the Isle of Man depend on the tourist trade for their livelihood. Similarly, other elements of recreation also have their own industrial remains to be examined.

The seaside is particularly full of industrial remains, many of which are quite old. The pier and pier railway certainly date from the early nineteenth century, and whilst they started with the more utilitarian purpose of giving access to and from pleasure vessels which brought visitors to the resorts, they quickly had further buildings added to them to provide entertainment and refreshment.

The fairground and the funfair also have an industrial past. Most fairground equipment was originally steam driven, and is now driven electrically by electricity generated in a mobile diesel generator. The permanent fairground, which occurs at many seaside resorts and in some of our larger towns, has much more rigid structures in the form of the Scenic Railway and the Tunnel of Love. Perhaps Copenhagen's Tivoli is the best known of these permanent structures, but there are equivalents in Battersea Park,

London, and the Spanish City, Whitley Bay. The mechanism of
scenic railways and the other forms of whirling, excitement-
inducing equipment would warrant a study in itself. The architecture, which is always of the impermanent lath and plaster, backcloth
type, falls into several patterns, and, with the gaudy painting
which always occurs, should be recorded.

One of the biggest industries of the entertainment world is that
of the cinema. In early days the camera was such a big piece of
equipment that it could not go on location and was confined to the
studio. This was a glass-walled greenhouse type of structure which
let in the maximum amount of light. The studio of Heinrich Her-
kommer in Bushey still exists and typifies this period. The next
family of studios are those where large stages were permanently
built in which the sets could be erected, used and demolished. The
offices and processing laboratories were attached to the front of
these to act as a noise screen from the road. The range at Denham,
Buckinghamshire, is an example of this type. Now most work
takes place away from the studios and all that is needed is a processing laboratory.

The theatre and the cinema which grew out of it are now becoming better documented. However, there is quite a large gap in our
recording of this industry as the music hall, which was one of the
transition points, and its successor, the silent cinema, were not
recorded while they existed. Now, early cinema buildings have been
converted to other uses and have lost their identity. The rectangular
hall with a projection booth and all the chimneys at high level
existed in many minor communities up and down the country and
has now ceased to be used at all. The Corn Exchange at Alnwick
in Northumberland was a typical cinema of the rectangular hall
type. Two huge cloisonné vases flanked the proscenium curtain
and were filled with real bullrushes. The seats were in part Finnish
bentwood with basket chairs at the rear of the flat floor for wealthier
patrons. Cinemas are, surprisingly, still being built, but they have

Plate 11. Wooden crane, still at Burbage Wharf, Kennet & Avon Canal, dated 1832

Plate 12. Engraving of wharf crane on quayside at Liverpool, circa 1830

Plate 13. Pontrhydefen Viaduct, Port Talbot Railway, Glamorgan. One of the last nineteenth-century brick railway viaducts

Plate 14. Back of the wing wall of an aqueduct by John Rennie on the Lancaster Canal. Photographed during demolition for road widening

ceased to have 2,000 seats and often are only sloping floors without galleries and have only 600 to 1,000 seats.

In the foregoing section some attempt has been made to show what industrial archaeologists are covering in their researches and fieldwork. The list is by no means complete, and the industrial archaeologist will find that his own coverage of the subject broadens as he explores further in his studies and fieldwork.

CHAPTER EIGHT

Conclusions

THE basic purpose of this volume has been to take the industrial archaeologist through the various facets of the discipline of this young subject. In the fifteen or so years that the subject has been growing, various factors have emerged which influence the industrial archaeologist in his choice of activity. The most important factor is that of urgency in view of the tremendous rate at which the visible elements of our industrial past are being erased by development. Though the products may not change, the processes of production have frequently changed, in some cases on the same site, and this alteration of method is now happening at an ever-increasing rate. It is important, therefore, to set out the priorities so that the industrial archaeologist may enjoy working in the discipline and at the same time contribute to the knowledge and preservation of our industrial history.

At the present time, the subject of industrial archaeology is so new that many areas of the country have few people working in them, and it is often necessary for the industrial archaeologist to commence work on his own with no one to whom to refer. For such a worker it is possibly best to join one of the many weekend or longer study courses held up and down the country by the extra-mural departments of the universities, before he becomes too deeply involved in the subject. In this way he can learn at first hand many of the techniques which have been set out in the preceding chapters. Possibly more important than this, is meeting with other workers and learning from them of the various activities in which they are involved. In other areas there are frequently WEA adult education courses held throughout the winter with summer activities in the field.

Students in other disciplines are now being given the opportunity to follow industrial archaeology as a subject in some universities. This has the advantage of giving some of the theoretical studies, such as economic history and geography, the firm background of work in the field. In the case of engineering and architecture, the background knowledge of the main subject is often assisted by the study of the history of industrial buildings and of machines. It is hoped, however, that the correct proportion of research and fieldwork can be maintained. It is rare for our knowledge of industrial techniques or history to be in any way increased by long lists of the 'Old Testament' type which identify the previous owners of industrial units without giving any clues to their status, ability, or economic standing. The scale of the subject is now so huge that there must be a continuing interdependence between students and part-time industrial archaeologists. Neither side of the discipline can eclipse the other, but they must work together to bring about greater knowledge of our industrial past and ensure its preservation or its adequate documentation in our records.

The work done in the field is of the greatest assistance to others. On the one hand fieldwork can be a guide to future planning problems by settling preservation priorities, and on the other hand it is the basis for further studies of industrial history and technology. It is in the field that the part-time industrial archaeologist can make his greatest contribution. Libraries and record offices are rarely open when he has his spare time, and so he is naturally inclined to spend more time in the field. It is on the records of existing plant and buildings that the preservation policies have to be built.

At the present time too little is known about the total remains of any one industry for the whole of that industry's remains to be examined item by item and a policy of preservation to be determined. Some people hold that the present remains of an industry should be preserved in their entirety. This view is quite unrealistic for there is not the money to support the preservations, nor would the public interest be sustained, as everything would become so commonplace. At the present time, however, the various monuments of our industrial heritage have to be examined on their own merits as the full extent of the industry to which they belong will not have been documented, nor the number of its monuments recorded.

If, for example, one looks at the possibility of the preservation of water-driven corn-mills, one is faced with an enormous problem of choice and justification. If one takes the present number of known watermill sites in Northumberland—300 plus—then it is statistically likely that England and Wales contain 10,000 sites of watermills. It is quite likely that there are 500 watermills which still contain their equipment, though this is not necessarily in good condition. If one were to discount mills which are privately preserved and not open to the public, then the probable number of mills which should be preserved and supported by the public is possibly reduced to one, or at the most two, per county, that is, about 100 mills. This leaves many mills at risk which should have some measure of protection so that they cannot easily be destroyed or their presence in our landscape lost.

The present legal protection of buildings, whether architectural or industrial, falls into two classes; one under the Ancient Monuments Acts, the second under the Planning Acts. The first is the responsibility of the Secretary of State for the Environment (in the section which was formerly the Ministry of Public Building and Works). Under the Ancient Monument Acts, a historic building is 'scheduled', and under the Planning Acts it is 'listed'. The selection of buildings to be placed on the schedules is the responsibility of the Ancient Monuments Board. When a building is scheduled, protection is afforded by the fact that the owner has to give three months' notice if he wishes to alter any part of the building. Because a building has been scheduled it is acknowledged that it is of national importance and that the preservation of its features is essential. It will be appreciated that the number of scheduled industrial monuments is quite small. The schedule also contains those industrial monuments which are in the guardianship of the Department of the Environment, such as Saxtead Green and Berney Arms Windmills, though many others are open to view such as the iron bridge at Ironbridge, and Tickford Bridge, Newport Pagnell, because they are in use.

The protection of the Planning Acts is given to buildings by recording them on lists of buildings of special architectural or historic interest. Again, these are the responsibility of the Secretary of State for the Environment (in the section which was formerly the Ministry of Housing and Local Government). The Secretary was required, under the various Planning Acts, to compile lists of buildings of special historic or architectural interest. In the mid-sixties the scope of these lists was extended to include industrial buildings, and, in some measure, their equipment. The listing is in three categories; Grade I—buildings of outstanding national importance; Grade II—buildings of special interest, the more important examples of which are Grade II* (known as Grade II star). Grade III buildings are those with some merit, either on their own or as part of a group. Grade I and Grade II buildings are protected by the fact that planning applications concerning them are dealt with at the local Planning Offices, but are also reviewed within two months by the Department of the Environment and certain nominated and concerned bodies. This affords some measure of protection, but it is no guarantee that the future of the building is assured. There is always a threat to buildings whether they are scheduled or listed, because of the tremendous pressure there is for land in this country, but in many cases this threat can be averted by the legal protection afforded by the Ancient Monuments and Planning Acts.

The last few years have seen an acceleration in the erosion of our industrial heritage by all forms of development, whether it be the property developer or the national road policy. It is therefore important that the recording of our industrial buildings proceeds as quickly as possible, and that the number of industrial archaeologists who are at work is increased. In the first instance, a simple photograph and an NRIM card should suffice; then if the monument is not of a type with which the industrial archaeologist is familiar, someone who has more knowledge can make a further record more fully. In this way particular buildings can be identified and their relative importance determined. Clearly, there are certain monuments which stand outside the normal scope of an industry and which have a uniqueness which justifies their preservation. The iron bridge at Ironbridge and Chesterton Windmill, Warwickshire, fall into this class. For the remainder, there are varying criteria which will justify the pursuit of either scheduling or listing. Is the monument typical of the normal production processes of its industry or its use? If not, is it the first unit which has survived, or is it the work of a particularly notable engineer? The Royal Albert Bridge at Saltash would fall into the latter category. The question of feasibility will also come into the problem. Will the monument be readily accessible to the public? If the monument is likely to be subject to vandalism because of its situation, is there any point in preserving it, particularly if other similar monuments exist in the area?

When preservation is contemplated, there are several approaches available to the industrial archaeologist or group. A preservation proposition is more likely to succeed when there is a willing team of volunteers to do a large amount of the work and to ensure future maintenance and control of the monument. In the first instance, since the industrial archaeologist or group is unlikely to own the building, it is important to establish a good arrangement with the owner. In many cases the owner has a concern for the monument, but cannot press for its preservation for financial or personal reasons.

The group will then be able to provide the effort neces, ary to preserve the monument. In such cases the owner may feel able to grant a lease at a nominal rent, or he may give the monument to the group. If this is the method of achieving preservation, a Trust should be formed to proceed with the work, and the future support of the monument. A Trust should be representative of local concerns and of the people who are able to help, whether with money, labour or materials. When the Trust is well established and plans are drawn up for the work of preservation, then a public appeal should be launched to get funds. At this stage, when the genuineness of the proposition is established, money should be sought from the local authority or the Historic Buildings Council, as well as from grant-giving Trusts. Examples of voluntary preservation can be seen at Wrawby Windmill, Lincolnshire, Chesterton Windmill, Warwickshire, and Nutley Windmill, Sussex. The work of the Northern Mill Engine Society and the Ryhope Pumping Engines Preservation Society are examples of the voluntary preservation of steam engines. Some museums also have teams of volunteers working in various aspects of the museum's activities, such as collecting, cataloguing, cleaning and preserving. One strong group works with the Oxford City and County Museum at Woodstock, doing fieldwork, measured drawings, and helping to preserve and maintain the 1847 steam engine at Combe Sawmill on the Blenheim estate.

Nationally, there is a great need for a concerted effort on the part of industrial archaeologists, and to help this movement they need to be more closely in touch with each other than has been the case in the past. Local groups need to work together to establish priorities for work in their areas. Whilst the process of preservation within the bounds of the present legislation is adequately dealt with under the existing arrangements of the Council for British Archaeology, a national movement needs to grow so that there is concerted effort in the right fields, and so that there is no clash of interests. A national movement should absorb the various types of worker in the discipline; university students and staff, the museum bodies, and the part-time industrial archaeologist. In bringing the variety of interests together it should be recognized that each has a great deal to give and receive, on an equal basis, from the other. Only in this way will the industrial archaeologist be able to get the greatest enjoyment from his discipline and make the greatest contribution to the preservation of our industrial heritage.

CHAPTER NINE

Museums

THE purpose of this chapter is to introduce the industrial archaeologist to the museums which will be of use to him in the extension of information on his chosen subject. Again, when in a particular area, he may wish to visit local museums and industrial monuments, and it is hoped that this list will help him.

There are several museums of national standing, such as the Science Museum, the Railway Museums and the National Museums of Scotland and Wales, which have large collections both on display and in reserve. A great number of museums are of more recent foundation, and, in consequence, their collections are still small. No attempt has been made in this list to differentiate between the size of the collections.

As there are some 1,000 museums in the country as a whole, only those with some relevance to industrial archaeology are listed. It must be borne in mind that some unlisted museums and galleries have a wealth of topographical pictures, water colours and engravings which can fill in the background of an area. Perhaps the best example of this is the collection of water colours and drawings belonging to the Laing Art Gallery in Newcastle-upon-Tyne, where this collection illustrates the whole range of industry and life in the north east.

Several companies have their own private museums related to their own history or their own particular industry. Perhaps the finest of these is the Pilkington Glass Museum at St Helens which was deliberately added to the new complex of offices when these were rebuilt in the sixties. Company museums are listed separately so that the user of the list can make arrangements for access, as their opening times are not normally given in the published directories of museums.

AEROPLANES AND AERONAUTICS

LONDON, *The Imperial War Museum*, Lambeth Road, SE1.

LONDON, *The Science Museum*, South Kensington, SW7.

LONDON COLNEY, Hertfordshire, *The Prototype De Havilland Mosquito*, Salisbury Hall.

OLD WARDEN, Bedfordshire, *The Shuttleworth Collection.*

YEOVILTON, Somerset, *Fleet Air Arm Museum.*

AGRICULTURE AND RURAL CRAFTS

ABERYSTWYTH, *University College of Wales: Museum and Art Gallery.*

ALTON, Hampshire, *The Curtis Museum*, High Street.

BANGOR, *Museum of Welsh Antiquities*, University College of North Wales, College Road.

BRIGHTON, *Brighton Museum and Art Gallery*, Church Street.

CAMBRIDGE, *Cambridge and County Folk Museum*, Castle Street.

DOUGLAS, Isle of Man, *The Manx Museum.*

EDINBURGH, *National Museum of Antiquities Annexe*, 18 Shandwick Place.

EVESHAM, Worcestershire, *The Almonry Museum*, Vine Street.

GLAMIS, Angus, *The Angus Folk Collection*, Kirkwynd.

GUERNSEY, *Guille Alles Museum*, St Peter Port.

KEIGHLEY, Yorkshire, *Keighley Art Gallery and Museum*, Cliffe Castle.

KIDDERMINSTER, *Worcestershire County Museum*, Hartlebury Castle, near Kidderminster.

LACOCK, Wiltshire, *Lackham College of Agriculture.*

NORWICH, *Bridewell Museum of Local Industries and Crafts*, Bridewell Alley.

READING, *Museum of English Rural Life*, Whiteknights Park.

SALISBURY, *Salisbury and South Wiltshire Museum*, St Anne Street.

SELKIRK, *Selkirk Museum*, Ettrick Terrace.
STROUD, Gloucestershire, *Stroud Museum*, Lansdown.
WILMINGTON, Sussex, *Wilmington Museum*, Wilmington Priory.
WYE, Kent, *Agricultural Museum*, Wye College.

COMPANY MUSEUMS

BIRMINGHAM, *The Assay Office*, Newhall Street, Birmingham 3 (gold and silversmithing).
BIRMINGHAM, *Avery Historical Museum*, Soho Foundry (history of weighing).
CAMBORNE, Cornwall, *Holman Bros. Museum*, Trevenson Street (mining and mining machinery).
COALBROOKDALE, Shropshire, *Allied Ironfounders* (now part of the Ironbridge Gorge Museum).
DUBLIN, *Guinness Museum* (brewing).
LONDON, *Chartered Insurance Institute Museum*, 20 Aldermanbury, EC2 (fire fighting etc).
LONDON, *ITA Television Gallery*, 70 Brompton Road, SW3 (television).
LONDON, *Kodak Museum*, Wealdstone, Harrow (photography and cinematography).
ROCHDALE, *Rochdale Co-operative Museum*, Toad Lane (the co-operative movement).
ST HELENS, Lancashire, *Pilkington Glass Museum*, Prescot Road.
ST MARY CRAY, Kent, *The National Paper Museum*.
STOKE-ON-TRENT, *The Wedgwood Museum*, Barlaston (china).
STOKE-ON-TRENT, *Spode-Copeland Museum and Art Gallery* (china).

ENGINEERING

DARLINGTON, *Darlington Museum*, Tubwell Row.
ECCLES, Lancashire, *Monks Hall Museum*, 42 Wellington Road.

GLASGOW, *City of Glasgow Corporation Art Gallery and Museum*, Kelvingrove.

GREENOCK, Renfrew, *The McLean Museum*, 9 Union Street, West End.

LIVERPOOL, *City of Liverpool Museums*, William Brown Street.

LONDON, *The Science Museum*, South Kensington, SW7.

NEWCASTLE-UPON-TYNE, *Museum of Science and Engineering*.

WEST HARTLEPOOL, *Gray Art Gallery and Museum*.

FOLK MUSEUMS

AYLESBURY, Buckinghamshire, *Buckinghamshire County Museum*, Church Street.

BEAMISH, County Durham, *North of England Open Air Museum*, Beamish Hall.

BELFAST, *Ulster Folk Museum*, Cultra Manor, Craigavad.

BRISTOL, *Blaise Castle House Museum*, Henbury.

CAMBRIDGE, *Cambridge and County Folk Museum*, 2 & 3 Castle Street.

CREGNEASH, Isle of Man, *Manx Village Folk Museum*.

DUBLIN, *National Museum of Ireland*, Kildare Street.

FILKINS, near Lechlade, Oxfordshire, *Filkins and Broughton Poggs Museum*.

FORT WILLIAM, *The West Highland Museum*, Cameron Square.

GAINSBOROUGH, Lincolnshire, *Gainsborough Old Hall*, Parnell Street.

GLAMIS, Angus, *The Angus Folk Collection*, Kirkwynd.

GLOUCESTER, *Bishop Hooper's Lodging*, 99 Westgate Street.

HALIFAX, Yorkshire, *West Yorkshire Folk Museum*, Shibden Hall, Shibden Park.

HELSTON, Cornwall, *Helston Borough Museum*, Old Butter Market.

KENDAL, Westmorland, *Abbot Hall Museum of Lakeland Life and Industry*.

KINGUSSIE, Inverness, *The Highland Folk Museum*.

LEEDS, *Abbey House Museum*, Kirkstall.
RUFFORD, Lancashire, *Rufford Old Hall*.
ST FAGANS, near Cardiff, *Welsh Folk Museum*.
STOWMARKET, Suffolk, *The Abbot's Hall Museum of Rural Life of East Anglia*.
TAUNTON, *Somerset County Museum*, Taunton Castle.
WEST DEAN, Sussex, *Weald and Downland Open Air Museum*.
WOODSTOCK, Oxfordshire, *The Oxford City and County Museum*, Fletcher's House.
YORK, *York Castle Museum*, Tower Street.
ZENNOR, Cornwall, *Wayside Museum*, Old Millhouse.

INDUSTRIAL

ABERDEEN, *The Industrial Museum*.
BEAMISH, County Durham, *North of England Open Air Museum*, Beamish Hall.
BIRMINGHAM, *Birmingham City Museum, Department of Science and Industry*, Newhall Street, Birmingham 3.
CARDIFF, *National Museum of Wales, Industrial Section*.
ECCLES, Lancashire, *Monks Hall Museum*, 42 Wellington Road.
GLASGOW, *City of Glasgow Corporation Art Gallery and Museum*, Kelvingrove.
LONDON, *The Science Museum*, South Kensington, SW7.
SWANSEA, *Industrial Museum of South Wales*, Victoria Road.
WEST HARTLEPOOL, *Gray Art Gallery and Museum*.
WHITBY, Yorkshire, *Whitby Museum*, Pannett Park.

METAL WORKING

BATTLE, Sussex, *Battle Museum*, Langton House.
BILSTON, Staffordshire, *Bilston Museum*, Mount Pleasant.
COALBROOKDALE, Shropshire, *Museum of Ironfounding*, Ironbridge Gorge Museum.

DUDLEY, *Dudley Museum and Art Gallery*, St James's Road.
FORT WILLIAM, *The West Highland Museum*, Cameron Square.
KEIGHLEY, Yorkshire, *Art Gallery and Museum*, Cliffe Castle.
LEWES, Sussex, *Anne of Cleeves House*, High Street, Southover.
REDDITCH, Worcestershire, *Forge Mill.*
SHEFFIELD, *Abbeydale Industrial Hamlet*, Abbeydale Road South.
SHEFFIELD, *Shepherd Wheel*, Whiteley Wood.
STICKLEPATH, Okehampton, Devon, *Finch Foundry.*
WORTLEY, Yorkshire, *Wortley Top Forge.*

MINING

BEAMISH, County Durham, *North of England Open Air Museum*, Beamish Hall.
CAMBORNE, Cornwall, *The Camborne School of Metalliferous Mining Museum.*
CAMBORNE, *Holman's Engineering Museum.*
IRONBRIDGE, Shropshire, *Ironbridge Gorge Museum*, Blists Hill.
KESWICK, *Fitz Park Museum and Art Gallery*, Station Road.
LOOE, Cornwall, *The Cornish Museum*, Lower Street, East Looe.
NEWCASTLE-UPON-TYNE, *Museum of Science and Engineering.*
NEWCASTLE-UPON-TNYE, *Museum of the Department of Mining Engineering*, The University, Queen Victoria Road.
PENZANCE, Cornwall, *Penzance Natural History and Antiquarian Museum*, Penlee Park.
SALFORD, Lancashire, *Science Museum*, Buile Hill Park.
ZENNOR, Cornwall, *Wayside Museum*, Old Millhouse.

RAILWAYS

BANGOR, Caernarvon, *Locomotive Museum*, Penrhyn Castle (National Trust).
BELFAST, *Transport Museum*, Witham Street, Newtownards Road.

DERBY, *Derby Museum and Art Gallery*, Strand.

GLASGOW, *Museum of Transport*, 25 Albert Drive, S1.

LEICESTER, *Railway Museum*, London Road, Stoneygate.

LONDON, *The Science Museum*, South Kensington, SW7.

PORTMADOC, Caernarvon, *Festiniog Railway Museum*.

STOCKTON, *Stockton and Darlington Railway Museum*.

SWINDON, *Great Western Railway Museum*, Farringdon Road.

TOWYN, Merioneth, *The Narrow Gauge Railway Museum*, Wharf Station.

YORK, *Railway Museum*, The Old Railway Station.

SHIPPING

ANNAN, Dumfries, *Annan Museum*, Moat House.

BARROW-IN-FURNESS, *Barrow-in-Furness Museum*, Ramsden Square.

BEAULIEU, Hampshire, *Maritime Museum*, Buckler's Hard.

BIRKENHEAD, *Williamson Art Gallery and Museum*, Slatey Road.

BRIXHAM, *Brixham Museum*, Higher Street.

CASTLETOWN, Isle of Man, *Nautical Museum*, Bridge Street.

DUNDEE, *Barrack Street Museum*, Ward Road.

EASTBOURNE, *Royal National Lifeboat Institution Museum*, Grand Parade.

EXETER, *Maritime Museum*, The Quay.

GLASGOW, *City of Glasgow Corporation Art Gallery and Museum*, Kelvingrove.

GOSPORT, *Submarine Museum*, HMS Dolphin.

GREAT YARMOUTH, *Maritime Museum for East Anglia*, Marine Parade.

GRIMSBY, *Doughty Museum*, Town Hall Square.

HULL, *Maritime Museum*, Pickering Park.

LITTLEHAMPTON, *Littlehampton Museum*, 12A River Road.

LIVERPOOL, *City of Liverpool Museums*, William Brown Street.

LONDON, *The National Maritime Museum*, Romney Road, Greenwich, SE10.

LONDON, *The Science Museum*, South Kensington, SW7.

LONDON, *The Cutty Sark and Gipsy Moth IV*, Greenwich Pier, SE10.

NEWCASTLE-UPON-TYNE, *Museum of Science and Engineering*.

PETERHEAD, Aberdeenshire, *Arbuthnot Museum*, St Peter Street.

PORTSMOUTH, *The Victory Museum*, HM Dockyard.

SOUTHAMPTON, *Maritime Museum*, Wool House, Bugle Street.

SOUTH SHIELDS, County Durham, *South Shields Library and Museum*, Ocean Road.

STOKE BRUERNE, Northamptonshire, *Waterways Museum*.

WHITBY, *Whitby Literary and Philosophical Museum*, Pannett Park.

STEAM POWER

BLAGDON, Somerset, *Blagdon Pumping Station*, Bristol Waterworks Company.

CAMBORNE, Cornwall, *Cornish Mine Beam Engines*, preserved by the Cornish Engines Preservation Society. These exist at South Crofty, Pool, near Redruth; East Pool and Agar Mine, Pool; Levant Mine.

CAMBRIDGE, *Cheddar's Lane Pumping Station*.

COMBE, Oxfordshire, *Combe Saw Mill*, the estate saw mill of the Marlborough Estate.

CROFTON, Wiltshire, *Crofton Beam Pumping Engines*.

DARTMOUTH, Devon, *The Newcomen Memorial Engine*, a preserved and re-erected Newcomen engine.

HOLLINWOOD, Lancashire, *The Ferranti Engines*.

PORTSMOUTH, *Eastney Sewage Pumping Station*.

ROCHDALE, Lancashire, *Dee Mill Engines*, Shaw. An in-situ preservation by the Northern Mill Engine Society. Further engines will be on view at Musgrave number 3 Mill, Mornington Road, Bolton.

ROTHERHAM, *Elsecar Pumping Engine*, a Newcomen-type engine.
SUNDERLAND, *Ryhope Pumping Station.*

TEXTILES

BATLEY, Yorkshire, *Bagshaw Museum*, Wilton Park.
BLACKBURN, *'Lewis' Textile Museum.*
BOLTON, Lancashire, *Tonge Moor Textile Machinery Museum*, Tonge Moor Road.
HALIFAX, *Bankfield Museum and Art Gallery*, Akroyd Park.
HAWICK, Roxburghshire, *Wilton Lodge Museum*, The Park.
HELMSHORE, Rossendale, Lancashire, *Higher Mill Museum.*
HONITON, Devon, *Honiton and Allhallows Public Museum*, High Street.
KILBRACHAN, Renfrew, *Weaver's Cottage*, The Cross.
LEICESTER, *Newarke Houses Museum*, The Newarke.
LEIGH, Lancashire, *Pennington Hall Museum and Art Gallery.*
LONDON, *Bethnal Green Museum*, Cambridge Heath Road.
LUTON, *Luton Museum and Art Gallery*, Wardown Park.
MACHYNLLETH, Montgomeryshire, *Plas Machynlleth.*
MANCHESTER, *Styles Cotton Industry Museum.*
PAISLEY, Renfrew, *Paisley Museum and Art Galleries*, High Street.

TRANSPORT

BEAULIEU, Hampshire, *The Montagu Motor Museum*, Palace House.
BELFAST, *Transport Museum*, Witham Street, Newtownards Road.
BROADWAY, *Snowshill Manor* (National Trust).
CHEDDAR, *Cheddar Motor and Transport Museum*, The Cliffs.
CRICH, near Matlock, Derbyshire, *The Tramway Museum*, Cliff Quarry, Crich.
GLASGOW, *Museum of Transport*, 25 Albert Drive, S1.
HUDDERSFIELD, *The Tolson Memorial Museum.*

HULL, *Transport and Archaeology Museum.*
LONDON, *The Science Museum,* South Kensington, SW7.
MAIDSTONE, *The Tyrwhitt-Drake Museum of Carriages,* Archbishop's Stables, Mill Street.
NEWCASTLE-UPON-TYNE, *Museum of Science and Engineering.*
NOTTINGHAM, *City Museum and Art Gallery,* The Castle.
OLD WARDEN, Bedfordshire, *The Shuttleworth Collection.*
SHUGBOROUGH, near Stafford, *Staffordshire County Museum and Mansion House.*

WATERMILLS AND WINDMILLS

Alford Windmill, Alford, Lincolnshire.
Arlington Watermill, Bibury, Gloucestershire.
Bembridge Windmill, Bembridge, Isle of Wight.
Berney Arms Windmill, Reedham, Norfolk. Note that at present this is reached only by train or boat.
Billing Watermill Museum, near Northampton.
Billingford Windmill, near Scole, Norfolk.
Bocking Windmill, near Braintree, Essex.
Bourn Windmill, Bourn, Cambridgeshire.
Brill Windmill, Brill, Buckinghamshire.
Brixton Windmill, Brixton, London.
Burgh-le-Marsh Windmill, Lincolnshire.
Calbourne Watermill, Newport, Isle of Wight.
Cheddleton Flint Mill, near Leek, Staffordshire.
Click Mill, Dounby, Orkney (a horizontal watermill).
Great Chishill Windmill, Cambridgeshire.
Haxted Watermill Museum, Edenbridge, Kent.
Heckington Windmill, Lincolnshire (eight-sailed).
Horsey Windmill, Norfolk.
Kentraugh Watermill, Colby, Isle of Man.
Lucton Watermill, Mortimers Cross, Herefordshire.

North Leverton Windmill, Nottinghamshire.
Nutley Windmill, Sussex.
Outwood Windmill, Surrey.
Pakenham Windmill, Suffolk.
Pitstone Windmill, near Ivinghoe, Buckinghamshire.
Preston Watermill, East Linton, East Lothian.
Sarehole Watermill, Warwickshire.
Saxtead Green Windmill, Suffolk.
Shipley Windmill, Sussex.
Stansted Mountfitchet Windmill, Essex.
Stevington Windmill, Bedfordshire.
Upminster Windmill, Essex.
Wrawby Windmill, near Brigg, Lincolnshire.

The opening times of the watermills and windmills listed above are much more restricted than those of museums. Visitors should find out when the mills are open before setting out.

Bibliography

THIS list of books has been completely revised as there have been a great many additions to the industrial archaeologist's library since 1966. In the field of regional studies, a lot of industrial archaeology is now included in what was previously local history and topographical description.

This bibliography is large because the editor feels that the books are appropriate to the study of industrial archaeology, and because they have been of value to him in the development of his knowledge of the subject. The industrial archaeologist should avail himself, through the use of secondhand bookshops or libraries, of the wealth of nineteenth-century technical literature when attempting to interpret the pattern of buildings and machines which he has found in the course of his fieldwork. Similarly, the industrial archaeologist should feel no shame in owning and using such early twentieth-century books as *The Childrens' Encyclopaedia* or *The Wonder Book for Boys*, as these can give a great deal of information, frequently in a simplified form, which is an aid to interpretation.

Whilst the list is built up under a series of headings, it contains each book only once. There are many books which are appropriate to the study of the subject under another heading, e.g. Robert Clough's *The Lead Smelting Mills of the Yorkshire Dales* which appears under the heading 'Metals', could equally well be referred to under 'Mining' or 'Watermills and Windmills'.

INDUSTRIAL ARCHAEOLOGY—GENERAL BOOKS

Buchanan, R. A. *Industrial Archaeology in Britain*, Penguin Books, 1972
Buchanan, R. A. (ed). *The Theory and Practice of Industrial Archaeology*, Bath University Press, 1968
Cossons, Neil and Hudson, Kenneth. *Industrial Archaeologists' Guide*, David & Charles, 1971 (published biennially)
Hudson, Kenneth. *Handbook for Industrial Archaeologists*, John Baker, 1967
Hudson, Kenneth. *Industrial Archaeology, an Introduction*, John Baker, 2nd ed, 1966

Hudson, Kenneth. *A Guide to the Industrial Archaeology of Europe*, Adams & Dart, 1971

Raistrick, Arthur. *Industrial Archaeology, an Historical Survey*, Eyre Methuen, 1972

Richards, J. M. and de Maré, Eric. *The Functional Tradition*, Architectural Press, 1958

Smith, Norman A. F. *Victorian Technology and Its Preservation in Modern Britain*, Leicester University Press, 1970

INDUSTRIAL ARCHAEOLOGY—REGIONAL STUDIES

ashmore, Owen. *The Industrial Archaeology of Lancashire*, David & Charles, 1969

Banks, A. G. and Schofield, R. B. *Brindley at Wet Earth Colliery, an Engineering Study*, David & Charles, 1968

Bawden, Garrad, Qualtrough and Scatchard. *The Industrial Archaeology of the Isle of Man*, David & Charles, 1972

Booker, Frank. *The Industrial Archaeology of the Tamar Valley*, David & Charles, 1967

Branch Johnson, W. *The Industrial Archaeology of Hertfordshire*, David & Charles, 1970

Buchanan, Angus. *Bristol, Industrial History in Pictures*, David & Charles, 1970

Buchanan, Angus and Cossons, Neil. *The Industrial Archaeology of the Bristol Region*, David & Charles, 1969

Butt, John. *The Industrial Archaeology of Scotland*, David & Charles, 1967

Butt, John, Donnachie, Ian and Hume, John R. *Scotland, Industrial History in Pictures*, David & Charles, 1968

Curnow, W. H. *Industrial Archaeology of Cornwall*, Tor Mark Press, 1969

Donnachie, Ian. *The Industrial Archaeology of Galloway*, David & Charles, 1971

Enfield Archaeological Society. *Industrial Archaeology in Enfield*, Enfield Archaeological Society, 1971

Green, E. R. R. *The Industrial Archaeology of County Down*, HMSO, 1963

Harris, Helen. *The Industrial Archaeology of Dartmoor*, David & Charles, 1968

Harris, Helen. *The Industrial Archaeology of the Peak District*, David &
Charles, 1971.
Hudson, Kenneth. *The Industrial Archaeology of Southern England*,
David & Charles, 1965
Marshall, J. D. and Davies-Shiel, M. *The Industrial Archaeology of the
Lake Counties*, David & Charles, 1969
Marshall, J. D. and Davies-Shiel, M. *The Lake District at Work*, David
& Charles, 1971
Nixon, Frank. *The Industrial Archaeology of Derbyshire*, David & Charles,
1969
Smith, David M. *The Industrial Archaeology of the East Midlands*,
David & Charles, 1965
Todd, A. C. and Laws, Peter. *The Industrial Archaeology of Cornwall*,
David & Charles, 1972
Wren, Wilfred I. *The Tanat Valley*, David & Charles, 1968
Wilson, Aubrey. *London's Industrial Heritage*, David & Charles, 1967

AGRICULTURE

Darby, H. C. *The Draining of the Fens*, Cambridge University Press, 1940
Evans, George Ewart. *The Horse in the Furrow*, Faber & Faber, 1960
Evans, George Ewart. *Where Beards Wag All—the Relevance of the Oral
Tradition*, Faber & Faber, 1970
Higgs, John. *The Land*, Studio Vista, 1964.
Hughes, W. J. *A Century of Traction Engines*, David & Charles, 1971
Russell, W. M. S. *Man, Nature and History*, Aldus Books, 1967
Vince, John. *Discovering Carts and Wagons*, Shire Publications, 1970
Wood, Emma and Hawke, Peter. *Our Agricultural Heritage—a Selection
of Farm Machinery Restored*, Esso, 1971

BIOGRAPHY

Boucher, Cyril T. G. *James Brindley Engineer, 1716–1772*, Goose, 1968
Boucher, Cyril T. G. *John Rennie, 1761–1821*, Manchester University
Press, 1963
Clements, Paul. *Marc Isambard Brunel*, Longmans, 1970
Harris, L. E. *Vermuyden and the Fens*, Cleaver Hume Press, 1953
Layson, J. F. *Great Engineers*, Walter Scott, c 1880
Pole, William. *The Life of Sir William Fairburn, Bart.*, 1877, reprinted
David & Charles, 1970

Raistrick, Arthur. *Quakers in Science and Industry*, 1950, reprinted David & Charles, 1972
Raistrick, Arthur. *Dynasty of Ironfounders*, 1953, reprinted David & Charles, 1970
Richardson, A. E. *Robert Mylne, Architect and Engineer*, Batsford, 1955
Rolt, L. T. C. *Isambard Kingdom Brunel*, Longmans, 1957
Rolt, L. T. C. *Thomas Newcomen, the Prehistory of the Steam Engine*, David & Charles, 1963
Rolt, L. T. C. *Thomas Telford*, Longmans, 1958
Rolt, L. T. C. *The Cornish Giant (Richard Trevithick)*, Lutterworth, 1960
Rolt, L. T. C. *Victorian Engineering*, Penguin Press, 1970
Rolt, L. T. C. *James Watt*, Batsford, 1962
Smiles, Samuel. *The Life of George Stephenson*, John Murray, 3rd ed, 1857
Smiles, Samuel. *The Life of Thomas Telford, Civil Engineer*, John Murray, 1867
Tames, Richard, *Isambard Kingdom Brunel*, Shire Publications, 1972
Vale, Edmund. *The Harveys of Hale*, Bradford Barton, 1966

BUILDING

Arkell, W. J. *Oxford Stone*, Faber & Faber, 1947
Barley, M. W. *The House and Home*, Studio Vista, 1963
Barley, M. W. *The English Farmhouse and Cottage*, Routledge & Kegan Paul, 1961
Becher, Bernard and Hilda. *Anonyme Skulpturen, Eine Typologie Technischer Bauten*, Art-Press Verlag, 1970
Brunskill, R. W. *Illustrated Handbook of Vernacular Architecture*, Faber & Faber, 1970
Clifton-Taylor, Alec. *The Pattern of English Building*, Batsford, 1962
Hewett, C. A. *The Development of Carpentry, 1200–1700*, David & Charles, 1969
Hudson, Kenneth. *Building Materials*, Longmans, 1972
Hudson, Kenneth. *The Fashionable Stone*, Adams & Dart, 1971
Innocent, C. F. *The Development of English Building Construction*, 1916, reprinted David & Charles, 1971
Peate, Iorwerth C. *The Welsh House*, Liverpool University Press, 1940
Searle, Alfred S. *Modern Brickmaking*, Scott Greenwood & Son, 1911
Smith, J. T. and Yates, E. M. *The Dating of English Houses from External Evidence*, reprinted from Field Studies, vol 2, no 3, 1968

M

Tann, Jennifer. *The Development of the Factory*, Cornmarket, 1970
Taylor, Nicholas. *Monuments of Commerce*, Country Life, 1968
Winter, John. *Industrial Architecture*, Studio Vista, 1970

CANALS AND RIVERS

Clew, Kenneth R. *The Kennet and Avon Canal*, David & Charles, 1968
De Maré, Eric. *The Canals of England*, Architectural Press, 1950
De Maré, Eric. *Time on the Thames*, Architectural Press, 1952
De Salis, H. R. *Bradshaw's Canals and Navigable Rivers of England and Wales*, 1904, reprinted David & Charles, 1969
Edwards, Lewis A. *Inland Waterways of Great Britain and Northern Ireland*, Imrey, Laurie Norie & Wilson, 1950
Gagg, John. *Canals in Camera*, Ian Allan, 1970
Hadfield, Charles. *British Canals, an Illustrated History*, Phoenix House, 1950
Hadfield, Charles. *The Canal Age*, David & Charles, 1968
Hadfield, Charles. *The Canals of South Wales and the Border*, Phoenix House, 1960
Hadfield, Charles. *The Canals of South and South East England*, David & Charles, 1969
Hadfield, Charles. *The Canals of South West England*, David & Charles, 1967
Harris, Robert. *Canals and Their Architecture*, Evelyn, 1969
Household, Humphrey. *The Thames and Severn Canal*, David & Charles, 1969
Priestley, Joseph. *Priestley's Navigable Rivers and Canals*, 1831, reprinted David & Charles, 1969
Spencer, Herbert. *London's Canal*, Putnam, 1961
Vine, P. A. L. *London's Lost Route to the Sea*, David & Charles, 1965
Vine, P. A. L. *London's Lost Route to Basingstoke*, David & Charles, 1968
Waterways Heritage, Luton Museum and Art Gallery, 1971

CIVIL ENGINEERING

Berridge, P. S. A. *The Girder Bridge after Brunel and Others*, Robert Maxwell, 1969
Crosby, Theo. *The Necessary Monument (Tower Bridge)*, Studio Vista, 1970
De Maré, Eric. *Bridges of Britain*, Batsford, 1954

Hopkins, H. J. *A Span of Bridges*, David & Charles, 1970
Matheson, Ewing. *Works in Iron* (Bridge and Roof Construction), Spon, 1873
Pannell, J. P. M. *An Illustrated History of Civil Engineering*, Thames & Hudson, 1964
Straub, Hans. *A History of Civil Engineering*, Leonard Hill, 1952
The Turnpike Age, Luton Museum and Art Gallery, 1971

CRAFTS

Arnold, James. *The Shell Book of Country Crafts*, John Baker, 1968
Hartley, Dorothy. *The Countryman's England*, Batsford, 2nd ed, 1942
Hennell, Thomas. *The Countryman at Work*, Architectural Press, 1947
Husa, Vaclav. *Traditional Crafts and Skills*, Paul Hamlyn, 1967
Jenkins, J. Geraint. *Traditional Country Craftsmen*, Routledge, 1965
Jenkins, J. Geraint. *The Craft Industries*, Longmans, 1972
Pullbrook, Ernest C. *English Country Life and Work*, Batsford, 1922
Rose, Walter. *The Village Carpenter*, Cambridge University Press, 1937
Sturt, George. *The Wheelwright's Shop*, 1923, reprinted Cambridge University Press, 1963
Wymer, Norman. *English Country Crafts*, Batsford, 1946
Wymer, Norman. *English Town Crafts*, Batsford, 1949

INDUSTRIAL HISTORY

Ashton, T. S. *The Industrial Revolution 1760–1830*, Oxford University Press, 1970
Burstall, Aubrey F. *A History of Mechanical Engineering*, Faber & Faber, 1963
Challoner, W. H. and Musson, A. E. *Industry and Technology*, Studio Vista, 1963
Chambers, J. D. *The Workshop of the World, British Economic History 1830–1880*, Oxford University Press, 1961
Chapman, S. D., Chambers, J. D. and Sharpe, T. R. *The Beginnings of Industrial Britain*, University Tutorial Press, 1970
Chapman, S. D. *The Early Factory Masters*, David & Charles, 1967
Cunningham W. and McArthur, Ellen A. *Outlines of English Industrial History*, Cambridge University Press, 1898
Dawson, Keith. *The Industrial Revolution*, Pan Books, 1972

Derry, T. K. and Williams, Trevor I. *A Short History of Technology*, Oxford University Press, 1960

Engineering Heritage, Highlights from the History of Mechanical Engineering, Institute of Mechanical Engineers, 1963 & 1966

Gibbins, H. D. *The Industrial History of England*, Methuen, 1890

Gille, Bertrand. *The Renaissance Engineers*, Lund Humphries, 1966

Harvie, Christopher, Martin, Graham and Scharf, Aaron, *Industrialisation and Culture, 1830–1914*, Open University, 1970

Henderson, W. O. *The Industrialization of Europe, 1780–1914*, Thames & Hudson, 1969

Hodges, Henry. *Technology in the Ancient World*, Penguin Books, 1970

Horne, A. E. *The Age of Machinery*, Blackie, 1913

Keller, A. G. *A Theatre of Machines*, Chapman & Hall, 1964

Klingender, Francis D. *Art and the Industrial Revolution*, edited and revised by Sir Arthur Elton, Evelyn, Adams & Mackay, 1968

Lardner, Dionysius. *The Museum of Science and Art*, 4 vols, Walton & Mabberley, 1854

Owen, W. and Bowen, E. *Wheels*, Time-Life Books, 1967

Quennell, Marjorie and C. H. B. *A History of Everyday Things in England*, 4 vols, Batsford, 1934

Rolt, L. T. C. *Tools for the Job*, Batsford, 1965

Singer, Charles and others. *A History of Technology*, 5 vols, Oxford University Press, 1954–1958

Singleton, Fred. *The Industrial Revolution in Yorkshire*, Dalesman, 1970

Tomlinson, Charles. *Cyclopoedia of Useful Arts, Manufactures, Mining and Engineering*, 2 vols, George Virtue, 1854

Wilson, Mitchell. *American Science and Inventions, a Pictorial History*, Bonanza, New York, 1960

LOCAL HISTORY AND RELATED STUDIES

Beresford, M. W. and Joseph, J. K. S. *Mediaeval England, an Aerial Survey*, Cambridge University Press, 1958

Bond, Maurice. *The Records of Parliament*, Phillimore, 1964

Crawford, O. G. S. *Archaeology in the Field*, Phoenix, 1953

Hoskins, W. G. *Local History in England*, Longmans, 1959

Hoskins, W. G. *The Making of the English Landscape*, Hodder & Stoughton, 1963

Hoskins, W. G. *Fieldwork in Local History*, Faber & Faber, 1967
Storey, R. L. *A Short Introduction to Wills*, Phillimore, 1966

MAPS AND GUIDES

Bowen, Emanuel and Kitchin, Thomas. *The Royal English Atlas*, 1762, reprinted David & Charles, 1972
Bowen, Emanuel. *Britannia Depicta*, 1720, reprinted Frank Graham, 1970
Brabner, J. H. F. (ed). *The Comprehensive Gazetteer of England and Wales*, William McKenzie, c 1900
Camden, William. *Camden's Britannia*, 1695, reprinted David & Charles 1971
Cary, John. *The Great Roads of England and Wales*, G. & J. Cary, 9th ed, 1821
Gazetteer of Great Britain (names of places shown on the quarter-inch series maps), Ordnance Survey
Lobel, M. D. (ed). *Historic Towns vol 1*, Lovell Johns—Cook, Hammond & Kell, 1969
Mason, Oliver. *A Gazetteer of England*, 2 vols, David & Charles, 1972
Mogg, Edward (ed). *Paterson's Roads*, Mogg, 18th ed, 1831
Morden, Robert. *The County Maps from William Camden's Britannia*, David & Charles, 1972
Ogilby, John. *Britannia*, 1675, reprinted Duckham, 1939

METALS

Clough, Robert T. *The Lead Smelting Mills of the Yorkshire Dales*, R. T. Clough, Leeds, 1962
Gale, W. K. V. *The British Iron and Steel Industry*, David & Charles, 1967
Gale, W. K. V. *The Black Country Iron Industry*, The Iron and Steel Institute, 1966
Hofman, H. O. *The Metallurgy of Lead*, The Scientific Publishing Co, New York, 1899
Lister, Raymond. *Decorative Cast Ironwork in Great Britain*, G. Bell & Sons, 1960
Straker, Ernest. *Wealden Iron*, 1931, reprinted Library Association—Chivers, 1967
Turner, Thomas. *The Metallurgy of Iron*, Griffin, 1895

MINING

Agricola, Georgius. *De Re Metallica*, 1556, trans. Herbert Hoover, 1912, reprinted Dover, New York, 1950
Atkinson, Frank. *The Great Northern Coalfield 1700–1900*, Durham Local History Society, 1966
Barton, D. B. *A History of Copper Mining in Cornwall and Devon*, Bradford Barton, 1968
Barton, D. B. *Essays in Cornish Mining History*, Bradford Barton, 1968
Down, C. G. and Warrington, A. J. *The History of the Somerset Coalfield*, David & Charles, 1971
Earl, Bryan. *Cornish Mining*, Bradford Barton, 1968
Ford, T. D. and Rieuwerts, J. H. *Lead Mining in the Peak District*, Peak Park Planning Board, 1968
Galloway, Robert L. *A History of Coal Mining in Great Britain*, 1882, reprinted David & Charles, 1969
Hair, T. H. *Sketches of the Coal Mines of Northumberland and Durham*, 1844, reprinted David & Charles, 1969
Hamilton, J. R. and Lawrence, J. F. *Men and Mining in the Quantocks*, Town & Country Press, 1970
Hughes, Herbert W. *A Text-Book of Coal Mining*, Griffin, 1893
Hunt, C. J. *The Lead Mines of the Northern Pennines in the Eighteenth and Nineteenth Centuries*, Manchester University Press, 1970
Ilseng, M. C. and Wilson, Eugene B. *A Manual of Mining*, John Wiley, New York, 1905
Kirkham, Nellie. *Derbyshire Lead Mining*, Bradford Barton, 1968
Morgan Rees, D. *Mines, Mills and Furnaces*, HMSO, 1969
North, F. J. *Mining for Metals in Wales*, National Museum of Wales, 1962
Raistrick, Arthur and Jennings, Bernard. *A History of Lead Mining in the Pennines*, Longmans, 1965
Shaw, W. T. *Mining in the Lake Counties*, Dalesman, 1972
Williams, Archibald. *The Romance of Mining*, C. Arthur Pearson, 1905

MUSEUMS

Atkinson, Frank. *Industrial Archaeology, Top Ten Sites in North East England*, Frank Graham, Newcastle, 1971
Cooksey, A. J. A. *British Museums of Interest to the Industrial Archaeologist*, Poole WEA Industrial Archaeology Group, 1968

Morgan, Bryan. *Railway Relics*, Ian Allen, 1969
Museums and Galleries in Great Britain and Ireland, ABC Travel Guides Ltd (an annual publication)
Sharp, Paul and Hatt, E. M. *Museums*, National Benzole Books, 1964
Treasures of Britain, Drive Publications Ltd, 1968

PHOTOGRAPHY

Allsopp, Bruce and Clarke, Ursula. *Photography for Tourists*, Oriel Press, 1966
De Maré, Eric. *Photography*, Penguin Books, 1957
De Maré, Eric. *Photography and Architecture*, Architectural Press, 1961
Matthews, S. K. *Photography in Archaeology and Art*, John Baker, 1969

POWER

Barton, D. B. *The Cornish Beam Engine*, Bradford Barton, 1965
Dickinson, H. W. *A Short History of the Steam Engine*, 1938, reprinted Cass, 1963
Jamieson, Andrew. *A Text Book of Steam and Steam Engines*, Griffin, 1886
Lewis, Paul. *The Romance of Water Power*, Sampson Low, c 1930
O'Brien, Robert. *Machines*, Time-Life, 1969
Passell, Carroll W. *Early Stationary Steam Engines in America*, Smithsonian Press, 1969
Rankine, W. J. M. *A Manual of the Steam Engine and Other Prime Movers*, Griffin, 1859
Watkins, George. *The Stationary Steam Engine*, David & Charles, 1968
Watkins, George. *The Textile Mill Engine*, 2 vols, David & Charles, 1970

PREPARATION OF REPORTS AND PAPERS

Bracegirdle, Brian. *Photography for Books and Reports*, David & Charles, 1970
Ginsell, L. Y., Rahtz, P. and Warhurst, A., *The Preparation of Archaeological Reports*, John Baker, 1966
Hart's Rules for Compositors and Readers, Oxford University Press, 37th ed, 1970
Hill, Adrian. *How to Draw*, Pan Books, 1963

Hodgkiss, A. G. *Maps for Books and Theses*, David & Charles, 1972
Parkinson, A. C. *A First Year Engineering Drawing*, Pitman, 6th ed, 1958
Thomas, David St John. *Non-Fiction: A Guide to Writing and Publishing*,
David & Charles, 1970

RAILWAYS

Baxter, Bertram. *Stone Blocks and Iron Rails*, David & Charles, 1966
Carmichael, J. W. *Views of the Newcastle and Carlisle Railway*, Frank
Graham, 1969
Coleman, Terry. *The Railway Navvies*, Hutchinson, 1966
Dendy Marshall, C. F. *A History of British Railways Down to the Year
1830*, 1938, reprinted Oxford University Press, 1971
Jennings, Paul. *Just a Few Lines*, Guinness Superlatives, 1969
Lewis, M. J. T. *Early Wooden Railways*, Routledge & Kegan Paul, 1970
Meeks, Carroll V. *The Railway Station*, Architectural Press, 1956
Smithson, A. and P. *The Euston Arch*, Thames & Hudson, 1968
Snell, J. B. *Mechanical Engineering: Railways*, Longmans, 1971
Tomlinson, W. W. *North Eastern Railway, Its Rise and Development*,
1914, reprinted David & Charles, 1967

REGIONAL STUDIES

Addy, John. *A Coal and Iron Community in the Industrial Revolution*,
Longmans, 1969
Aikin, J. *A Description of the Country from Thirty to Forty Miles round
Manchester*, 1795, reprinted David & Charles, 1968
Atthill, Robin. *Old Mendip*, David & Charles, 1964
Bick, D. E. *Old Leckhampton*, D. E. Bick, Cheltenham, 1971
Brill, Edith. *Old Cotswold*, David & Charles, 1968
Finberg, H. P. R. *Gloucestershire, an Illustrated Essay on the History of
the Landscape*, Hodder & Stoughton, 1955
Hart, Cyril. *The Industrial History of Dean*, David & Charles, 1971
McCord, N. and Rowe, D. T. *Northumberland and Durham, an Industrial
Miscellany*, Frank Graham, 1971
Millward, R. *Lancashire, an Illustrated History of the Landscape*, Hodder
& Stoughton, 1955
Millward, R. and Robinson, A. *The Lake District*, Eyre & Spottiswoode,
1970
Pannell, J. P. M. *Old Southampton Shores*, David & Charles, 1967

Bibliography 191

Raistrick, Arthur. *The Pennine Dales*, Eyre & Spottiswoode, 1968
Raistrick, Arthur. *Old Yorkshire Dales*, David & Charles, 1967

SERVICE INDUSTRIES

Binnie, Alex R. *Water Supply, Rainfall, Reservoirs, Conduits and Distribution*, W. & J. Mackay, 1887
D'Acres, R. *The Art of Water Drawing*, 1660, reprinted Newcomen Society, 1930
Davies, Selwyn. *Fresh Water*, Aldus Books, 1967
Dickinson, H. W. *Water Supply of Greater London*, Newcomen Society, 1954
Hartley, Dorothy. *Water in England*, Macdonald, 1964
Hornby, John. *A Text Book of Gas Manufacture for Students*, G. Bell & Sons, 1913
Leopold, Luna B. and Davis, Kenneth S. *Water*, Time-Life Books, 1970

WATERMILLS AND WINDMILLS

Armengaude, Aine. *Moteurs Hydraulique*, vol I, text, *Atlas Hydraulique*, vol II, Paris, 1868
Batten, M. I. *English Windmills*, vol 1, Architectural Press, 1932
Bennett, Richard and Elton, John. *History of Cornmilling*, 4 vols, Simpkin Marshall & Co, 1899
De Molens in Brabant, Dienst voor Geschiedkundige en Folkloristische Opzoekingen van de Provincie Brabant, 1961
Bruggeman, Jean. *Nos Moulins (Flandres, Hainault, Cambresis)*, Actica Editions, Lille, 1972
Coles Finch, W. *Watermills and Windmills* (the windmills of Kent), C. W. Daniel, 1933
Farries, K. G. and Mason, M. T. *The Windmills of Surrey and Inner London*, Charles Skilton, 1966
Freese, Stanley. *Windmills and Millwrighting*, David & Charles, 2nd ed, 1971
Hartley, E. N. *Ironworks on the Saugus*, University of Oklahoma Press, 1957
Hills, R. L. *Machines, Mills and Uncountable Costly Necessities*, Goose, 1967
Jespersen, Anders. *Gearing in Watermills*, Virum, Denmark, 1953

Jespersen, Anders (ed). *Report on Watermills, Volume Three*, (a large volume of measured drawings), Virum, 1957
Jespersen, Anders. *Windmills on Bornholm*, Virum, 1958
Jespersen, Anders (ed). *Transactions of the Second International Symposium of Molinology*, Copenhagen, 1969
Little, R. J. de. *The Windmill, Yesterday and Today*, John Baker, 1972
Lockwood, J. F. *Flour Milling*, Northern Publishing Co, Liverpool, 3rd ed, 1952
Major, J. Kenneth. *The Mills of the Isle of Wight*, Charles Skilton, 1970
Minchinton, Walter and Perkins, John. *Tidemills of Devon and Cornwall*, Exeter Papers in Industrial Archaeology, 1972
Pallett, Henry. *Miller's, Millwright's and Engineer's Guide*, Henry Carey Baird & Co, Philadelphia, 1878
Reynolds, John. *Windmills and Watermills*, Evelyn, 1970
Short, Michael. *Windmills in Lambeth, an Historical Survey*, London Borough of Lambeth, 1971
Skilton, C. P. *British Windmills and Watermills*, Collins, 1947
Skilton, Charles. *Windmills and Watermills in Water-Colour*, The Old Water-Colour Society's Club, 40th annual volume, 1965
Smith, Donald. *English Windmills*, vol 2, Architectural Press, 1932
Somervell, John. *Water-Power Mills of South Westmorland*, Titus Wilson, Kendal, 1930
Stokhuyzen, Frederick. *The Dutch Windmill*, Merlin Press, 1962
Storck, John and Teague, Walter Donvin. *Flour for Man's Bread*, University of Minnesota Press, 1952
Studtje, Johannes. *Mühlen in Schleswig-Holstein*, Boyens & Co, Heide in Holstein, 1968
Syson, Leslie. *British Watermills*, Batsford, 1965
Tann, Jennifer. *Gloucestershire Woollen Mills*, David & Charles, 1967
Van Natrus, Leendert and Polly, Jacob. *Groot Volkomen Moolenboek*, Amsterdam, 1734, reprinted Van Kampen, Amsterdam, 1969
Wailes, Rex. *The English Windmill*, Routledge & Kegan Paul, 2nd ed, 1967
Wailes, Rex. *Windmills in England*, Architectural Press, 1948
Wailes, Rex and Marshall, Bernice. *The Mills of Long Island*, Ira J. Friedman, Long Island, New York, 1962
Wolff, Alfred R. *The Windmill as Prime Mover*, John Wiley & Sons, New York, 2nd ed, 1894

JOURNALS

The industrial archaeologist will find articles on various aspects of his subject in many magazines and newspapers. Magazines such as the weekly *Country Life* and the quarterly *Countryman* frequently contain articles, notes and letters on industrial archaeological subjects, and newspapers occasionally carry articles or letters with illustrations, of some threatened building or industrial process.

For the dedicated industrial archaeologist, the quarterly *Industrial Archaeology: The Journal of the History of Industry and Technology*, is published on a subscription basis by David & Charles. This publishes articles by research workers and others engaged in fieldwork, and is the best means of keeping up to date in all that is under way in this important discipline.

Since 1966, many industrial archaeology societies have been formed, and their newsletters, bulletins and journals contain articles on research and fieldwork of a high standard. Particularly notable regional productions are *The Newsletter of the Gloucestershire Society for Industrial Archaeology, The North-East Industrial Archaeology Society Bulletin, Sussex Industrial History, Industrial Archaeology in Wales Newsletter*, and *Wiltshire Industrial Archaeology*. Details of these societies and their publications can be found in *Industrial Archaeologists Guide*, published by David & Charles.

The *Transactions* of the Newcomen Society for the study of the history of engineering and technology are published annually from the headquarters of the society at the Science Museum, London, SW7. All members of the society receive the *Transactions*; the published price to non-members being the same as the subscription to the society. In the forty-two volumes published up to 1972, a great number of authoritative papers have been included, and most, if not all, of these are on subjects which may properly be described as industrial archaeology.

Acknowledgements

THE author of a book such as this must draw on many outside resources and, in the present instance, he has availed himself over many years of the kindness of friends and acquaintances too numerous to mention here.

There are, however, some whose contributions call for special thanks. They include members of the University of Southampton, particularly Mr H. J. Sara, BSc, who assisted in measuring at Eling Mill; Mr A. C. Clark, Chief Cartographer, Department of Geography, who gave valuable aid with Ordnance Survey reproductions; and Miss D. M. Marshallsay, BA, of the Ford Collection of Parliamentary Papers.

The librarians and staffs of the Library of Southampton University, the City Libraries and the Library of The Institution of Civil Engineers.

The City Archivist of Southampton, Edwin Welch, MA, not only assisted with Chapters Two and Three, but also contributed the section on Business Archives.

The Wardens and Fellows of Winchester College, through the Estates Bursar, Mr D. H. Vellacott, MA, very kindly allowed full facilities for measuring, photographing and generally exploring Eling Mill.

Miss Diane Angel, as usual, not only typed a very workmanlike script, but at the same time kept check on the author's style.

Finally, but most important of all, the author's wife, whose help and encouragement are always available in those times of crisis which inevitably occur at some stages of the preparation of a book such as this one.

Index